"My Dear Loraine"

"My Dear Loraine"

BERNARD SHAW'S LETTERS TO AN ACTOR

Edited by
L.W. Conolly

The Academy of the Shaw Festival

Distributed by Rock's Mills Press

Library and Archives Canada Cataloguing in Publication

Title: "My dear Loraine" : Bernard Shaw's letters to an actor / edited by L.W. Conolly.
Other titles: Correspondence. Selections
Names: Shaw, Bernard, 1856-1950, author. | Conolly, L. W. (Leonard W.), editor.
Description: Includes bibliographical references and index.
Identifiers: Canadiana 20190214740 | ISBN 9781775063223 (softcover)
Subjects: LCSH: Shaw, Bernard, 1856-1950—Correspondence. | LCSH: Loraine, Robert, 1876-1935—
   Correspondence. | LCSH: Dramatists, Irish—20th century—Correspondence.
Classification: LCC PR5366.A45 2020 | DDC 822/.912—dc23

First published in 2020 by
The Academy of the Shaw Festival
P.O. Box 774
Niagara-on-the-Lake, Ontario L0S 1J0
www.shawfest.ca

The letters of Bernard Shaw are © 2020 the Estate of Bernard Shaw and are published by kind permission of the Society of Authors on behalf of the Shaw Estate. All editorial matter is © L.W. Conolly.

No part of this publication may be reproduced or stored in a retrieval system, or transmitted in any form or by any means, electronic, mechanical, recording, or otherwise, without written permission of the publisher.

Designed by Aldo Fierro

Cover photo: Robert Loraine as Cyrano, 1919
Cover background: Old photographs © malerapaso@istockphoto.com

This edition distributed by Rock's Mills Press
ISBN 978-1-77244-187-1

For
Cecil John Layton Price (1915–1991)
In gratitude

CONTENTS

Acknowledgements • ix
Introduction • 1
Note on the Text • 7
Abbreviations • 9
The Shaw–Loraine Letters [*previously unpublished] • 11

1	6 January 1909* •	11
2	13 December 1914 •	14
3	14 January 1915 •	18
4	1 September 1915* •	21
5	25 July 1918 •	23
6	4 August 1918 •	25
7	9 August 1918 •	26
8	30 September 1918 •	29
9	19 April 1919 •	32
10	12 July 1919 •	34
11	14 December 1919 •	36
12	20 December 1919* •	42
13	16 January 1920* •	45
14	19 January 1920 •	47
15	8 January 1922* •	49
16	18 June 1922* •	52
17	18 July 1922* •	54
18	17 August 1922* •	56
19	16 January 1923* •	57

20	16 September 1926* •	59
21	9 October 1926* •	62
22	19 February 1928* •	63
23	20 July 1929 •	66
24	17 September 1932* •	68
25	14 April 1933* •	70

Notes • 73

Sources • 79

Index • 81

ACKNOWLEDGEMENTS

I again have the pleasure of thanking David Grapes II* for bringing to my attention previously unpublished Shaw letters, now held in his extensive private theatre collection, and for granting permission for their publication. This is the third book that has resulted from the commitment of David Grapes not only to seek out and acquire important Shaviana, but to make such acquisitions accessible through publication. The two previous books are *My Dear Loraine: Bernard Shaw's Letters to a Critic* (2017) and *Bernard Shaw's Postmistress: The Memoir of Jisbella Georgina Lyth as Told to Romie Lambkin* (2018). Both books are edited by L.W. Conolly, published by the Academy of the Shaw Festival (www.shawfest.com), and distributed by Rock's Mills Press (www.rocksmillspress.com).

Colleagues J.P. Wearing and Michel Pharand have provided valuable help with queries regarding annotations to the letters, and Michel has once more given extensively and generously of his time in reading and correcting drafts of this book. Also gratefully acknowledged are the interest and support of Shaw Festival Executive Director Tim Jennings, and Jen Rubio and David Stover of Rock's Mills Press.

And again I offer profuse thanks to family members for their expertise in proofreading (Barbara Conolly), editing (Rebecca Conolly), and design (Aldo Fierro).

*Emeritus Professor of Theater and Founding Director of the School of Theater Arts and Dance at the University of Northern Colorado, where he also served as the Producing Artistic Director for UNC's professional summer stock company (the Little Theater of the Rockies, founded in 1934), David Grapes has combined a distinguished teaching and administrative career with award-winning accomplishments as director, actor, drama critic, and playwright. He has provided artistic leadership and has directed and acted at major regional theatres across the United States, is creator or co-creator of several musical reviews and plays that have enjoyed national and international success, and for many years has reviewed plays at Canada's Shaw and Stratford Festivals for the Booth newspaper chain (Michigan), for other media outlets, and for his own online Canadian Theatre Festivals blog. David Grapes began collecting archival theatre materials in 1976, since when he has accumulated a rich research and teaching resource, with particular emphasis on Bernard Shaw and his contemporaries. Holdings in his collection include correspondence, cabinet cards, signed photographs, first editions, programmes, posters, recordings, scripts, ephemera, and memorabilia.

INTRODUCTION

The British actor Robert Loraine (1876–1935) was an important figure in Bernard Shaw's life, both personally and professionally. It was Loraine who successfully introduced *Man and Superman* (as John Tanner) to New York audiences in 1905 and subsequently to many other American and Canadian cities on tour. The New York premiere at the Hudson Theatre opened on 5 September 1905 and ran for 192 performances. Loraine also succeeded Harley Granville Barker as Tanner at the Royal Court Theatre in London in 1907 and, while playing Tanner in the evenings, also played Don Juan in the Don Juan in Hell scene at a series of matinees, thus becoming the first actor to have played both roles (though never in the full-length play). Loraine created the roles of St John Hotchkiss in *Getting Married* in 1908 and General Mitchener in *Press Cuttings* in 1909. He also regularly played—not always to Shaw's satisfaction—Bluntschli in *Arms and the Man*. Shaw was unequivocally impressed, however, by Loraine's Cyrano in a long run of *Cyrano de Bergerac* in London in 1919 and by Loraine's commitment later in his career to Strindberg's plays in London and on Broadway.

During the First World War, Loraine, a celebrated pioneer aviator, was a pilot in the fledgling Royal Air Force (then the Royal Flying Corps) and was twice seriously wounded. In 1914 shrapnel destroyed one of his lungs, and in the final year of the war in a battle with a German aircraft he was hit so badly in the left leg that surgeons recommended amputation. Eager to continue his acting career after the war, Loraine rejected the medical advice, but subsequent surgery, albeit saving his leg, left him with a distinctive limp—which he used to good effect as Cyrano, but otherwise was often an impediment he had to disguise on stage as best he could. Loraine was awarded both the Military Cross and the Distinguished Service Order for his war service.[1]

Before and after the war, Loraine was a frequent guest of Shaw and his wife Charlotte in London and in Ayot St Lawrence, and they sometimes holidayed together as well. On one such holiday—in Llanbedr in Wales in 1907—both men very nearly drowned while swimming in the ocean, a misadventure vividly described by Shaw in a letter to H.G. Wells.[2] By the outbreak of war in 1914, the relationship between Loraine and the Shaws was such that Loraine named them in his military files as next-of-kin, and when Loraine was awarded the Military Cross he sent it (and other valuables) to Shaw for safekeeping.[3] Shaw also loaned money to the often impecunious Loraine, and the Shaws attended his wedding in July 1921.[4] The three remained close throughout the 1920s and 1930s as Loraine criss-crossed the Atlantic in sometimes futile attempts to sustain a frequently spluttering acting career, Shaw never hesitant to offer guidance and support. Such letters, of course, also expose Shaw's own theatrical values, biases, and frustrations.

All biographies of Shaw treat to some extent his relationship with Loraine, but the two published biographies of Loraine go into much greater detail. The first, by Loraine's second wife, Winifred, was published in London (Collins) in 1938 as *Robert Loraine: Soldier, Actor, Airman*, and in New York (William Morrow) in 1939 as *Head Wind: The Story of Robert Loraine*. Winifred Loraine used three principal sources for her account of Loraine's relationship with Shaw:

her personal knowledge, Loraine's diary, and Shaw's many letters to Loraine. The second biography, *The Life of Robert Loraine: The Stage, the Sky, and George Bernard Shaw*, by historian Lanayre D. Liggera, was published in 2013. Liggera drew extensively on Winifred Loraine's biography and also interviews with one of Loraine's three daughters (Winifred died in 1986). Liggera also conducted extensive research in primary and secondary sources. Shaw scholars Dan Laurence and Stanley Weintraub assisted her, and Weintraub wrote the foreword to her book.

In her biography of her husband, Winifred Loraine—sometimes extensively, sometimes briefly—quotes from several letters, postcards, and cables from Shaw to Loraine. On Winifred's death, family papers, including Shaw's letters to Loraine, came into the possession of her daughter, Joan Loraine. Liggera revealed in her book, however (7), that "no further family papers" (beyond those quoted in the biography) "have been forthcoming" from Joan. However, shortly after Liggera's book was published, a collection of 69 Shaw–Loraine letters, postcards, and cables (including those quoted in Winifred Loraine's biography) were put up for auction by a dealer in Somerset, not far from Joan Loraine's home.[5] They failed to attract a buyer, and in the meantime Joan Loraine died; unmarried, she is survived by a niece and two nephews (*Daily Telegraph* obituary, 27 March 2016).

The collection, however, remained available from Joan Loraine's executors, and eventually (in 2018) was acquired by American collector David Grapes II to become part of his impressive theatre holdings. Grapes generously made the collection available for publication,[6] and it is with his permission, together with the permission of the Estate of Bernard Shaw, that 25 of the letters are published here. Fourteen of them (#s 1, 4, 12, 13, 15, 16, 17, 18, 19, 20, 21, 22, 24, 25) have never been previously published, in whole or in part. The remaining 11 are quoted by Winifred Loraine in her biography, with numerous omissions and inaccuracies, and are here included (again for the first time) in full and with the erroneous transcriptions corrected.[7]

While many of Winifred Loraine's mis-transcriptions are relatively minor, some significantly alter Shaw's meaning. For example, in his 13 December 1914 letter (#2), Shaw tells Loraine that he attended a concert in Torquay where he "led cheers" for wounded Belgian troops in the audience. Winifred Loraine's transcription of "led cheers" is "set chairs"—an error that is particularly difficult to fathom since Shaw's letter is typed and perfectly legible. Shaw's 9 August 1918 letter (#7) is handwritten, but still legible (as most of Shaw's handwriting is). But when Shaw is giving advice to Loraine about his leg wound (to amputate or not to amputate?), he asks about the pension implications: "How much for a leg? How much for a limp?" In Winifred Loraine's transcription this becomes, "How much for a leg? How much for limb?" And in the 14 December 1919 letter (#11), which largely has to do with Shaw's criticism of Loraine's recently opened production of *Arms and the Man* at the Duke of York's Theatre, when Shaw insists that the cast must ignore the audience, especially the laughter, by playing "deafly and blindly," Winifred Loraine makes it "deftly and blindly" (though the letter is again typed). In order to fit the flow and context of her narrative, she also omits sections of letters—sometimes a line or to, sometimes substantial paragraphs—without indicating it.

The letters selected for this edition[8] reveal many things about the Shaw–Loraine relationship, a relationship that, at times, bears an an uncanny resemblance to another Shavian military bond—that with T.E. Lawrence, Lawrence of Arabia. Twelve years Loraine's senior, Lawrence died in 1935 a few months before Loraine. Both men were treated by the Shaws as close to kin,[9] though in Loraine's case there was the added element (and sometimes complication) of balancing personal ties with professional priorities. Ever willing to support Loraine's acting and management career, Shaw was a firm but constructive (usually) critic of his acting (see his detailed letters [#s 11, 12] on Loraine's Bluntschli), and also of his management ventures (see letter #22 on Loraine's missteps at the Apollo Theatre). When he thought that Loraine was wasting his talents on dross (as he often was), Shaw didn't hesitate to say so. And he was constantly encouraging Loraine to expand his Shavian repertoire beyond Loraine's favoured Tanner and Bluntschli—Higgins (*Pygmalion*), Brassbound (*Captain Brassbound's Conversion*), and Burgoyne (*The Devil's Disciple*), for example. The first letter here is a good example of Shaw's financial acumen, an asset notably lacking in Loraine's skill set, while the succeeding letters, in various ways, complement, supplement, and correct what the Winifred Loraine and Lanayre Liggera biographies reveal about one of the most resilient and satisfying relationships in the lives of both men.

NOTE ON THE TEXT

With the exception of italicizing titles of plays, books, and Shaw's underlinings, and standardizing Shaw's often inconsistent practice with apostrophes, the transcription of the letters is true to the originals (including Shaw's sometimes idiosyncratic or arcane spelling).

ABBREVIATIONS

ALS   Autograph Letter Signed
BL   The British Library
CL   *Bernard Shaw, Collected Letters.* 4 vols., ed. Dan H. Laurence. New York: Viking Penguin, 1965–88.
PU   Previously unpublished
TLS   Typed Letter Signed

THE SHAW–LORAINE LETTERS

1   *Between their first meeting in London in 1905 and this letter from Shaw in early January 1909 (from the home of Charlotte Shaw's sister and her husband in the market town of Wem in Shropshire), Loraine had performed John Tanner in* Man and Superman *hundreds of times in America and England, had enjoyed a two-month run as Bluntschli in* Arms and the Man *at the Avenue Theatre in 1907–08, and had created the role of St John Hotchkiss in* Getting Married *at the Haymarket in May 1908. In July 1908 he had pitched to Shaw—unsuccessfully—the idea of a London season of his plays (CL 2:127), and then, it seems, priced himself out of the part of Cashel Byron in* The Admirable Bashville *at His Majesty's Theatre (part of Herbert Beerbohm Tree's "Afternoon Theatre" matinee series), despite being Shaw's first choice for the role. Ben Webster (1864–1947), who had created the role in the first professional production by the Stage Society in 1903, got the part again. The cast also included Marie Lohr (1890–1975) who played Lydia, Rosina Filippi (1866–1930) as Adelaine Gisborne, Henry Ainley (1879–1945) as Bashville, James Hearn (1873–1913) as Cetewayo, and Edward Sass (d.1916) as Paradise. Renowned Polish pianist Ignacy Jan Paderewski (1860–1941) was the exemplar held up by Shaw for financial reality among artists. (Throughout his relationship with Loraine, Shaw proved himself the more astute and pragmatic man of business.) Shaw's essay on Edgar Allan Poe was published in* The

Nation, *edited by Henry Massingham, on 16 January 1909. Britain's National Theatre, a project vigorously supported by Shaw, was not founded until 1963. The "Haymarket play" was Oliver Goldsmith's* She Stoops to Conquer, *in which Loraine played Young Marlow. It opened on 20 February 1909, but ran for only 25 performances, closing well before Easter.*

[ALS] [PU]

Edstaston Wem
Shropshire

6 January 1909

My dear Loraine

They tell me they have cast Webster (the original) for Cashel Byron. I told them to do so if they could not secure you.

Your blessed market terms are utter nonsense for repertory theatres. Padcrewski plays for the Philharmonic Society for about fifteen shillings, as all the great musical swells do, knowing that the Society cannot pay what you call market prices. These market terms depend on what you can draw. If the result of your playing is that there is £20 more in the house than there would be if the next best man were playing, then obviously you can ask & get £19-19-11¾ [19 pounds, 19 shillings, 11¾ pence] more than he, with a profit to the management of ¼d [a farthing]. If you stand out for £20-0-0¼, then the next best man gets the job. Taking our cast as it stands, with the author a star in himself, Marie Lohr, Rosina Filippi, Ainley the Beautiful, and Hearn as leading tragedian, the difference made by your playing Cashel instead of Ben Webster is, at the outside, about twopence. Sass as Paradise will be a far greater attraction. If you have asked your Haymarket terms, you have asked your own value instead of the value of the part. I don't say you are not right; but the effect is to cut you out of all engagements except those in which you can earn your salary, including every possible part at this Afternoon Theatre.

In my own case I have two prices: one for American magazines and the other for English ones, the proportion being as high as 8 to 1 or even much more. For instance I am writing an article on Poe for Massingham (*The Nation*), and shall take what he can afford—possibly nothing, possibly 12 guineas, at the utmost, £25. But for an American magazine I should expect up to £200.

When the National Theatre is established, every leading actor will have to give it the benefit of a special scale & play on it for honor & glory and a modest living wage, whilst keeping up commercial terms for people who are out for money & money alone. There is nothing wrong in two prices, if the conditions are different. Playing for nothing does not get over the difficulty: if you do that, you blackleg Webster. You should jealously keep up prices on the low scale as much as on the high scale. But the high scale is impossible for repertory or short run high class work. If Webster will play for, say, £5 a show (I have no idea of what his terms are) and you want £150, I can't honestly say that you will draw the difference; and I can't reasonably demand that the management should pay more than the part is worth.

I don't know whether they have actually engaged Ben; but he is in the cast sent me by Dana [unidentified] this morning. I can't complain: he did it very well before, and did it for nothing: in fact I behaved like a sweep in trying to get you. The refusal of the part was morally due to him.

What about America? Is the Haymarket play going to run until Easter?

I return to town on Friday morning, or possibly tomorrow evening. My host here yesterday mistook the accelerator pedal for the footbrake & drove my car at full speed up the front steps. The steps are wrecked & so is the steering & front axle of the car. But for this I should have driven up tomorrow. As it is I don't quite know what trains I shall come by.

G.B.S.

2   *Later in 1909, Loraine created the role of General Mitchener in* Press Cuttings *(at the Court on 9 July), and took on a number of non-Shavian roles in the West End. He returned to Shaw in September 1911 with a revival of* Man and Superman *at the Criterion. It ran for 167 performances, but still lost money, prompting Loraine to return to America in 1912 for more New York and touring productions of the play. ("He has been hard hit pecuniarily," Shaw wrote to Charlotte [19 April 1912,* CL *3:83].) When he returned to London in 1913, he continued to perform in the West End, but his appearance in Henry Arthur Jones's* The Silver King *at His Majesty's in May 1914 was his last before the war. Shaw in the meantime had premiered* Misalliance, Fanny's First Play, Androcles and the Lion, *and* Pygmalion, *and, in November 1914, had published his controversial* Common Sense About the War *(in which, among many other provocative comments, Shaw urged soldiers on both sides of the conflict to shoot their officers and return home), just a few weeks after Loraine had joined the Royal Flying Corps.*

Loraine was badly wounded in November 1914, causing concerted efforts by Shaw and Charlotte to find out from the War Office more about his condition and his whereabouts. The Uhlans that Loraine attacked from the air were enemy light cavalry, and the Bromo paper that Charlotte was advised to send Loraine was chemically treated (with bromides) toilet paper. The Belgian city of Louvain (Leuven) suffered severe damage throughout the war. The famous British forces song "It's a Long Way to Tipperary" was double Dutch to Belgian soldiers convalescing in England.

[TLS] [Loraine 10.1667 in99–201] [*CL* 3:278–80]

Ayot St Lawrence
Welwyn, Herts.

13 December 1914

My dear Loraine

Charlotte managed to track you down within twenty[-]four hours of your landing by a sustained frontal attack on the War Office and the Horse Guards. Before that we could hear nothing about you except legendary matter, mostly to the effect that instead of doing your duty by observing the enemy's position and bringing back reports, your habit was to charge the Uhlans with your aeroplane, at last driving [the] French to declare that if you were not speedily slain there would not be a serviceable flying machine left in the whole -----[10] army.

The first credible news was that you were hit: the next, that you had lost a lung. This alarmed me, because one of my uncles lost a lung, and though he recovered all his previous robustness of habit yet he died of it after lingering in this state for forty[-]seven years.

We called yesterday, but were informed by a sympathetic footman that you were not to see anybody. We wanted to see you for two special reasons.

1. To know whether there is anything you want that we can get you and send you, or anything that we can do that you want done. Charlotte made inquiries during your active service as to what ought to be sent to officers in the field. At the shops they knew all about it, and proposed silver[-]mounted dressing cases, dispatch

boxes, baths, roasting jacks, and armchairs. Then she asked men who had come back from the front. They all said "Bromo paper: nothing else; and disguise it as much as possible in the packing or it will be stolen." Such suggestions, though sensible, are the death of romance.

2. I wanted to see for myself how you were; for I knew that medical reports and diagnoses were worth nothing in the face of your powers of acting, and that it was just a toss-up whether you would be in the mood to wile away your last hour by a breezy cheerful "It's nothing: I shall be out again in a week," or, if you felt exceptionally full of beans, to treat them to a deathbed scene that would plunge the whole hospital into convulsive weeping. The Colonel of the Horse Guards (Peterkin was his martial name; and he was very nice to Charlotte) reported you as on the cheery tack, from which I apprehended the worst.

I hope, anyhow, that you are bad enough not to be allowed out again; for really you have done enough for honor, and there are plenty of fellows who will stop shrapnel quite as effectively as you and who are not useful to their country in other respects as you are. This war seems likely at present to last about fifteen years, at the end of which the million heroes engaged will have a sudden common inspiration. They will say simultaneously "This is a mug's game" and go home. Sic transit gloria mundi.

We are down at Ayot and shall be there until the middle or end of next week. I console myself for the bad weather by considering that it is important that you should be kept in the lowest spirits, as laughing cannot be good for shrapnel in the lung.

We have some Belgian wounded in this neighborhood. They keep up their spirits by telling lies, for which there is an unlimited popular demand. We all mourn the man who returned to the front last week. He was the man to whom a beautiful woman with her hands cut off by the Uhlans had said, holding up her bleeding stumps, "Remember me." I envy the *désinvolture* [casualness] of one who, having seen the real thing, can still amuse himself in that fashion.

For my own part, I have been giving exhibitions of moral courage far surpassing anything achieved in the field; but so far I have not received the V.C.:[11] in fact, sarcastic suggestions that I should receive the iron one[12] have not been lacking. However, you will find the papers rather less sanctimonious than they were before I gave their show away and substituted the trumpet for the harmonium as the martial instrument of Britain.

The situation of the British theatre is rather less eligible than that of Louvain at present; but the profession keeps alive by giving performances for the relief of the Belgians; also by reciting patriotic odes at the halls, the interest being kept up by announcements that the reciter is on 96 hours leave from the trenches. By this means he often secures an engagement for a whole fortnight.

I must stop now, as I am told that you should be written to gradually. I have tried to be as gradual as possible. Do not bother about acknowledging. The nurse can make a note of our telephone number 8131 City (it is not in the book). My secretary Miss [Ann] Elder, or Mrs [Margaret] Bilton the housekeeper, can take any message and send it on; or they can do anything you want.

We were down most of the time at Torquay, where I wrote my immortal *Common Sense About the War*, and led cheers at the Pavilion for the wounded Belgians. The band played *Tipperary* for these warriors, who, instead of rising on their crutches and bursting into enthusiastic cheers, made it only too clear by their dazed demeanor that they were listening to this inspiring tune for the first time in their lives.

ever,

G.B.S.

3 *A long convalescent voyage followed for the wounded Loraine, during which he planned to write a book about his flying experiences. He sought advice from Shaw (BL Add MS 50517 ff 2–3, 13 January 1914: "You see, I am rather torn and confused as to the Reader I want. . . . you do so often throw a flood of illumination on a difficulty"), who responded at considerable length about how he should write the book. Despite Shaw's guidance, however, it was never completed.*

[TLS signed] [Loraine 204–206]

10 Adelphi Terrace
London W.C.[2]

14 January 1915

My dear Loraine

It is very hard, without a regular professional experience of writing on a particular subject, to know how much space one's material will take. Matter that seems to fill up one's mind to the very limits of the universe boils down unexpectedly into three pages; and, on the other hand, details that are not foreseen at all in conceiving the book spread out to whole volumes. You will not know, until it comes to actual pen and ink, how much or how little of what you know and what you think can be turned to literary account.

You will find that before you can write a book on military aeroplaning, you will have to think about it. But you must be particularly careful not to write about it. This apparently idiotic remark is really a very sensible and important one. It all turns on the innocent word "about." You must get the actual thing down on paper, and avoid writing *about* it, or chronicling the process of thinking *about* it which you had to agonize through before you started. The public won't want to know how you got at your conclusions: it wants wants, first, to know what military aeroplaning is actually like; and not until it knows that, will it be interested in or be capable of following any argument or generalizing *about* it.

Therefore, if I had the job to do, I should start straight away with my diary. I should describe exactly what happens to a flier in the field from the moment he wakes up in the morning to the climax at which he is riddled with bullets four thousand feet up. I should describe roughly what has to be done to the machine before it is dragged out, and where it has passed the night, and how you get into it, and how much room there is for you in it, and whether you always have the same machine and the same pilot or whether you have to take your chance as with a taxi, and what clothes you have to wear, and all about the colored pencils stuck in your gloves, and the compass, and the aneroid, and the barograph,[13] and the stopwatch, and the sphygmograph (to record the jumps given by your heart when a shell bursts near you), and the stethoscope, and the bottle of hair dye (to conceal the ravages of terror), and the fountain pen, and the field glasses, and the goggles, and everything else that you carry as part of your equipment, or that the other fellow carries. Then I should describe the orders, and the officer you get them from, and the day's work mapped out for you. I should describe the business of spotting artillery positions, and of reconaissances. I should describe the descent, and the report, and the use made of the report: for instance, in the case of artillery positions, the sort of memorandum the officer to whom you report gives to the artillery officer, so as to set him firing in the air at something that not one of them except the flier has ever seen or ever will see.

All this will be very interesting, and exactly what the public want to know. It will also be technical in the way that the reader likes things to be technical: that is, intelligibly technical. Technical terms madden people when they don't understand them; but when the meaning is clear they like them, because they can repeat them in private conversation with an air of knowing all about it.

Next, I should go on from the things that happen every day as a matter of course, to the things that may happen at any moment, such as wounds, failure of engine, fogs, attacks by hostile aeroplanes, or catching sight of them and having to attack them, and, generally, what may be called adventures, including a statement not only of the things you have to do out of your own head in emergencies, but the things as to which you have permanent orders, such as attacking hostile aircraft at sight, or destroying your machine to prevent it from falling into enemies' hands. Also the routine of surrender, and, of course, the relations between the observer and the pilot, as far as this can be delicately done.

You can set to at all this without thinking about it. All you have to do is simply to recollect and trust to your native faculty for dramatic narrative without (for God's sake) any conscious exploitation of it. But by the time you have finished you will discover that you have been quite naturally led to think a lot about it all; and you will find yourself ready to go on to any theorizing and generalizing that may seem safe to you. You will not only have strategy and tactics, and the relative merits of flotated dirigibles and heavier-than-air-aircraft, with accounts of such duels between aeroplanes and zeppelins as you may have been engaged in or know about, but also a very interesting chapter on bomb dropping on towns. Everybody wants to know whether we shall have in future to live under bombproof shelters by electric light and never see the sun, or else to give up war. Incidentally you can go into the technique of bomb dropping.

That is how the matter arranges itself in my mind; and it is quite good enough to start on; for in the end the thing will arrange itself.

Now as to the business part. If you find your stuff easily divisible into sections and about 2000 words each, then your best course would be to offer it as a series of articles to *The Times*. If you proposed it to them, and submitted a couple of sample articles, they might quite possibly make you an offer for half a dozen under some such heading as "The flying man in the field" (it ought to be in the firmament, by the way), by Robert Loraine. You could then ask Paul Reynolds, 70 Fifth Avenue, New York, who is a capable agent for that sort of job, to arrange for simultaneous publication in some New York daily. If this succeeded, you would get money enough to pay for your ink to start with; and you could then collect the articles and make your book, which could contain such extra matter, if any, as would not have come under the head of practicable journalism.

This is all I can think at present. I doubt if you will be able to write much on board ship: I never can, though I can write almost anywhere else. However, you can try in the intervals of struggling with the Morse code.[14] And so, bon voyage.

Yours ever

G. Bernard Shaw

P.S. [*Handwritten by Shaw*] *Don't* write in any particular attitude, dignified or popular or otherwise. That will only lead to acting—in the sense in which you implore an actor at rehearsal not to act. Let it come just as it will naturally. Correcting its manners is a matter for revision on the proof: it is a matter of altering a word here and there to spare somebody's feelings, and does not affect one word in every thousand. All good style comes from being sincere and saying what you mean as exactly as possible.

4 *Having temporarily lost touch with Loraine, who had returned to active service in April 1915, Shaw tried to contact him from Torquay, where he and Charlotte were holidaying. The immediate*

issue for Shaw was Gertrude Kingston's (1866–1937) upcoming visit to America with Shaw's one-act plays Great Catherine *and* The Inca of Perusalem, *both of which opened at the Neighbourhood Playhouse in New York on 14 November 1916, but without Loraine, who was firmly committed to seeing out the war rather than returning to his theatrical career. Actor-director-playwright Harley Granville Barker (1877–1946) abandoned his theatre career when he met Helen Huntington, his future (second) wife in 1915, whom, after war service (and divorce from Lillah McCarthy), he married in 1918.*

[ALS] [PU]

The Hydro [Hotel]
Torquay

1 September 1915

[No salutation]

Art alive, man? We havn't the least idea.

Gertrude Kingston is going to America with my *Great Catherine*, and an anonymous new one-acter called *The Inca of Perusalem*, which I have reason to believe contains a part of great topical interest (the title part) equal to anything the stage has offered to a great actor for centuries. Patiomkin in *Catherine* is also Kolossal. Gertrude asks whether she cannot have you to double them. I can only reply that Heaven alone knows how many holes you have in you by this time.

Barker has forsworn the theatre and retired from management. In future he will write plays and think in continents. Meanwhile he is in khaki, reporting on hospitals for the Red Cross people, and probably watching the shrapnel bursting round you in the air.[15]

We are here in Torquay, bathing. I am having a splendid holiday—havn't done so much work for a long time past as I am getting through between my swims.

A sign of life from you, if only the official postcard, will be most welcome.

G.B.S.

5 *During the war, Shaw maintained intermittent contact with Loraine, who succeeded in avoiding further injury until the final summer of the conflict, when he was hit in the left leg and hip, not by "Archies" (British military slang for German anti-aircraft guns), but by machine-gun fire in aerial combat. That marked the end of Loraine's war service and the beginning of his difficult return to acting, though not, as Shaw might have hoped, in his new play,* Back to Methuselah.

[TLS] [Loraine 242]

10 Adelphi Terrace
[London] W.C.2

25 July 1918

My dear Loraine

I have just received an official telegram announcing that you have been and done it again, or rather the Huns have. It reached me just before lunch; and I had to keep it to myself until Charlotte had finished a solid meal, as it would certainly have put her badly off it if I had told her beforehand. We both find ourselves much concerned.

What is the use of being a major if you have to out yourself in the way of Archies like a common lieutenant?

I hope it is not as bad as last time, and cling rather to the fact that the telegram does not say seriously or dangerously wounded. "Reported wounded on July 20th[;] particulars to follow when received" is the wording. Anyhow, you are alive. I find myself repeating the lines from *Lear* [Edgar to Gloucester, IV.vi]

> Hadst thou been Gossamer! Feathers! Air!
> So many fathoms down precipitating,
> Thoudst shivered like an egg.

You would produce that impression by sheer dramatic power if you had only fallen two feet.

We are both on the point of starting for our annual holiday, I to various places in England, and Charlotte to Ireland. We shall be away probably until October. Therefore letters will take from one to three days longer to reach us than in London. [*This last sentence is Shaw's handwritten insertion.*]

I hope they will send those particulars soon and that it is a cushy one this time. You are going too far with this silly soldiering. I have written a play with intervals of thousands of years (in the future) between the acts, but now I find that I must make each act into a full[-]length play. And this is the time you select to stop another bullet!

The devil take the war!

Ever

G. Bernard Shaw

6 *Shaw received more news about Loraine's wounds while he was in Streatley (a village in Berkshire, about 90 km west of London), where he was sitting for a bronze sculpture by Lady Kathleen Scott (1874–1947), widow of Antarctic explorer, Robert Falcon Scott (1868–1912). The assumption at this stage was that Loraine's leg would have to be amputated, hence Lady Scott's recommendation for a prosthesis (ironically, of German origin, apparently not available from the specialist hospital in Roehampton, a district of southwest London—Shaw's own recommendation was a hospital in Bournemouth on the south coast). Shaw's reassurances to Loraine derive from a period in 1898 when an infection in his left foot led to surgery and several months on crutches. The bomber that Shaw refers to was manufactured by the Handley-Page Aircraft Company in 1916.*

[ALS] [Loraine 242–43]

Streatley (en voyage)

4 August 1918

My dear Loraine

News at last. Gunshot wound in the left knee joint. Lady Scott, who is making a statuette of me, and putting me up here for ten days (expiring tomorrow) accordingly, explains cheerfully "Oh, tell him to be sure not to take any leg they recommend at Roehampton," and proceeds to entertain me with stories of a friend of hers who got a proper Ernst leg, and who plays tennis, & bicycles with it, without giving it away. I trust it is not necessary to rush to conclusions in this fashion: still, if the worst comes to the worst I suppose one can play Hamlet with a property leg as well as lawn tennis. Why the devil need they have hit you in the knee joint? [T]he shin would have served their purpose just as well. (Apparently they *did*[.] 30/9/18)[16]

I spent eighteen months on crutches, unable to put my foot to the ground—left foot it was, too. But that period produced *Caesar & Cleopatra* & *The Perfect Wagnerite*; and I cannot remember that I was in the least less happy than at other times. After all, having two serviceable legs, I have never groused because I have not three; so why should the man with one be wretched because he has not two?

These are the cheering remarks one makes now to the sacrifices of this horrible war. They must make you long to bomb Britain from the newest Handley-Page.

Make them send you home to the orthopaedic hospital at Bournemouth as soon as possible: it is a mistake to suppose that one hospital is as good as another for this sort of thing.

A speedy deliverance to you!

ever

G. Bernard Shaw

7   *Shaw's 1918 summer holidays then took him to Presteigne in Wales, where he received further news of Loraine's medical situation. His reflections on the still-uncertain fate of Loraine's leg were both whimsical (he never did write a Byron play) and practical (pension implications). H.G. Wells's (1866–1946) Martian appears in his novel* War of the Worlds *(1898). Loraine continued (as a civilian) to fly after the war, but he made no attempt to follow Shaw's suggestion that he tackle a flight across the Atlantic (soon to be achieved for the first time—in June 1919—by British pilots John Alcock and Arthur Brown on a 16-hour flight from St John's in Newfoundland to Connemara in Ireland). Polish-born fighter pilot Manfred von Richthofen (1892–1918), the "Red Baron," was credited with 80 air combat victories for the German*

air force during the war. He was himself killed in in action on 21 April 1918. Shaw's caustic reference to Richthofen's "honor" draws on Falstaff's comment on Sir Walter Blunt in Shakespeare's Henry IV Part I, *IV.iii. Charles Ricketts (1866–1931) designed the costumes for Loraine's Don Juan in* Don Juan in Hell *at the Court Theatre in June 1907. He did so, said Shaw, "in a "very wonderful way" (CL 2:693). Founded by James McNeill Whistler in 1885, the International Society of Sculptors, Painters and Gravers was a professional organization that mounted exhibitions of work by its members in London and the provinces. Shaw had visited European battlefields in January 1917 at the invitation of Sir Douglas Haig, Commander-in-Chief of the British army, and had lived in London at 10 Adelphi Terrace since his marriage to Charlotte in 1898.*

[ALS] [Loraine 244–45] [CL 3:559–60]

at Dr Thelwall's[17]
Presteign[e]
Radnorshire

9 August 1918

My dear Loraine

Your letter of the 31st has just arrived. For Heaven's sake don't discourage the communicativeness of the Air Ministry: without it I should have had no news at all until today. Let them write and unburden their grief: what else have they to do?

I don't know what to say about the leg. If you lose it, an artificial leg of the best sort will carry you to victory as Henry V. If you dont, and are lame, it means a lifetime of Richard III, unless I write a play entitled *Byron*. Then there is the pension. How much for a leg? How much for a limp? One must look at these things from a business point of view. An ordinary man is more disabled by losing a leg than by laming it (and pensions proceed on that assumption); but an actor may be more disabled by a crooked leg than by a cork one. How about flying? It seems to me that when it comes to aerial combat the more of you that is artificial the better. Wells's Martian, a brain in a machine, is the ideal. You could carry spare limbs, and replace damaged ones whilst you are volplaning.[18] A dozen bullets through an artificial shin would move you to nothing but a Mephistophelean laugh.

If we did not die of laughter at the humors of war we should die of horror. Europe, in fact, *is* dying of horror to a considerable extent, though it does not know it.

The question is, what are you going to do when they set you on your legs? The first flight to America remains unachieved. You have done enough Richthofening for honor; and I like not such grinning honor as Richthofen hath. There still remains Columbus to emulate. You have, God forgive you, bombed enough German homesteads to fill ten pages of the Recording Angel's debit columns; and it behoves you to start a credit by drying up the Atlantic for ever. The world will be full of such jobs for bold men for a long time to come; and the expiatory soldier will find his chance in them. I no longer think of you as an actor except as a joke or a reminiscence.

Talking of that, Ricketts exhibited at the International so splendidly romantic a picture of Don Juan and the Statue that, stony broke as I am, I believe that I should have bought it and presented it to you if somebody had not got beforehand with me on the first day of the show and saved me £300. And the costume was not in the least like the elegant confection with which he clothed your radiant youth at the Court Theatre, but a luridly magnificent one of rich velvets of the sort you wanted. So the laugh is with you after all.

Perhaps this letter will reach Dunkirk after you have left. Try for Bournemouth: don't let them stick you in London now that nobody is there. Even if you had to overstay the holiday time you would have to balance the visits of your friends against those of the hovering Hun on the moonless nights. I have quite lost the iron nerve with which I faced the bombs of Ypres and Arras: the raids now terrify me into heart[-]rending palpitations; and I am too lazy to get up and go down to the excellent Adelphi cellars.

I must stop to catch the post.

ever

G. Bernard Shaw

8   *In the event, Loraine's leg was saved by Sir Alfred Fripp, a distinguished London surgeon, and he convalesced in Swanage, a coastal town in Dorset in the southwest of England (having moved there from Bryanston Sq., south of Regent's Park in the Marylebone district of London). Ruth Cavendish-Bentwick (1867–1953), a prominent suffragette, lived at Corfe Castle, about 10 km northwest of Swanage. Meanwhile, Shaw had joined Charlotte in Ireland, visiting Lady Augusta Gregory (1852–1932), co-founder with W.B.Yeats (1865–1939) of the Irish National Theatre Society, at her home in Coole Park, Gort, County Galway. Other visits were made to Charlotte's relatives in Lucan, near Dublin, one of whom—her sister Mary Cholmondeley (c1858–1929)—Loraine had met in the unlikely circumstance of a balloon flight in July 1906 (Liggera 72–73). Herbert Beerbohm Tree (1852–1917) had played Higgins opposite Mrs Patrick Campbell's (1865–1940) Eliza in the 1913–14 Haymarket Theatre premiere of* Pygmalion. *Nothing came of the idea of a Loraine–Campbell* Pygmalion, *though Mrs Campbell subsequently played Eliza again opposite C. Aubrey Smith at the Aldwych in 1920 (see letter 13). Shaw was right, however, in surmising that*

the permanent limp that resulted from the surgery on Loraine's leg would not necessarily restrict his acting career; he was soon to make a great success with Cyrano (letter 9). Henry Ainley (1879–1945) was a leading Shakespearean actor who had also created the role of the Bishop of Chelsea in Getting Married *at the Haymarket on 12 May 1908 (when Loraine had created the role of St John Hotchkiss).* Black Eyed Susan *was a popular melodrama by Douglas Jerrold, first performed in 1829.*

[ALS signed] [Loraine 246–47] [*CL* 3:565–66]

Parknasilla
[Kenmare
County Kerry]

30 September 1918

My dear Loraine

As it happened, all the missing correspondence was thrown back at me out of the blue in two instalments just before your letter arrived. It is all very stale; but I send it on.

We are packing for our departure tomorrow morning, and shall return to London via Limerick, Lady Gregory's, Capt Colthurst's (Mrs Colthurst is Charlotte's niece, daughter of Mrs Cholmondeley in the balloon), and home somewhere round about the 20th.

I am glad you are out of Bryanston Square: it is no place for a convalescent. If you come across Mrs Cavendish Bentwick (Corfe Castle), and feel seditious, claim me as a common friend, and talk treason to your heart's content.

How soon will you be able to play again if you decide to return to the boards instead of starting an Aeroplane Express? You can work controls with a game leg, can't you? It's only shoving a stretcher? The reason I ask is that as *Pygmalion* came off at His Majesty's at the end of the season to big business, and Tree was discussing a resumption of it when he died, Mrs Campbell is looking round for another go.[19] Now, there is not the least reason why Higgins shouldn't be lame, or Tanner lame, or any of the rest of my heroes. So long as you have a mouth left and one lung to keep it going, you will still be better than the next best: my pieces are not leg pieces. In fact the only parts you couldn't very well play are parts in which the character is supposed to be lame and has to make allusions to it. Which, by the way, knocks out my suggestion of Richard III—but you could omit the line and stick to the envious mountain on his shoulder. A limp may even be an asset: we shall have Ainley playing with one arm inside his waistcoat, and glass eyes dropping out into teacups in comic scenes: no unwounded need apply & so forth. William in *Black Eyed Susan* will dance the hornpipe on one wooden leg.

It is no joke, all the same; but quite seriously there is, when you come to think of it, no reason why an actor should, like a Roman Catholic priest, be perfect in all his members in order to discharge his function. A manager might jib at it at first; but when one appearance had settled the question by the play going through exactly as usual (except for a little extra sympathy to begin with) it would never be thought of again.

Let us know when you shift from Swanage. News of you meanwhile will always be welcome; but don't write duty letters to anyone: they will inflame the knee.

ever

G. B.S.

9   *Loraine returned to the stage on 28 March 1919 at the Garrick Theatre as Cyrano in Edmond Rostand's* Cyrano de Bergerac.[20] *Including transfers to Drury Lane, the Duke of York's, and the Savoy,* Cyrano *ran for 226 performances. Covent Garden had a bigger seating capacity (about 2,000) than all of them, except Drury Lane (about 2,500), but was typically used for grand opera, not drama. After creating the role of Cyrano in Paris in 1897, Benoît-Constant Coquelin (1841–1909) took the play to London in the summer of 1898, and subsequently (with Sarah Bernhardt as Roxane) toured it in the United States. By the end of the war Loraine had reached the rank of lieutenant-colonel—hence Shaw's reference to "the colonel." Oundle School, founded in 1556, is in Oundle, Northamptonshire. Shaw saw* Arms and the Man *there on 1 April 1919 with H.G. Wells, whose sons attended the school (Gibbs 233). Shaw's advice to Ada King (d 1940), who played the Duenna in Loraine's* Cyrano de Bergerac, *on how "tryst" should be pronounced has not stood the test of time.*

[TLS] [Loraine 260–61]

Ayot St Lawrence
Welwyn, Herts.

19 April 1919

My dear Loraine

I shall get into trouble with Charlotte for having gone to *Cyrano* without her; but I was in town on an emergency on Tuesday, and could not resist the opportunity of looking in. It is enchanting, and has the quite special quality that belongs to you in an extraordinary degree; but you should have taken Covent Garden to make it pay. It shews up Coquelin's Cyrano as a *tour de force* of method and execution rather than a moving embodiment of a dramatic poem. I enjoyed Coquelin with a connoisseur's enjoyment of his technique; but I was really moved by your playing, and delighted to find that the artist had killed the colonel and not the colonel the artist.

I had great misgivings about the play when I heard you were going to attempt it, because the difficulties of translation seemed to me insuperable. But the untranslatable bits (the ballades) don't matter so much as I thought: there is enough common human stuff in the play to make it independent of language.

I gather from the behavior of the box office that business is immense. They threw me a stall as they would throw a bone to a dog.

I suppose one must be careful not to fire shots in a shell shocked world; but I was at a performance of *Arms and the Man* at Oundle School the other day; and the school rifle corps did some of the most terrific shooting in the first act that even you ever heard at the front. In fact it was the making of the play. Perhaps it was this recent experience that made your drum taps sound unconvincing to me; but I think they are a bit underdone, especially the shot that kills Christian. Unless there are special reasons against it I urge a genuine fusillade.

Tell Ada King that tryst rhymes to Christ and not to whist.

Have you a revolving stage, that you work your changes so quickly?

At the end you must be careful of a very effective comic No that is one of your gifts. You exploded it once (inadvertently I think) in the very moving passage in the death scene where you deny that you loved Roxane.

Also, I don't think Cyrano should fall. The whole point of the death is that he dies on his feet; and he ought to stiffen there and be visibly a standing dead man. To make this clear[,] Roxane, not realizing that he is dead, should go to his assistance; and then the statue should fall, and fall stiff. To save your bones, one of the men, seeing what is happening, should catch him as he is falling away from her, and the two should let him down, still stiff as a poker, at full length. Just try it one or two ways. As it is, it is too obviously a stage fall; and the effect of the scene is so very fine that it is a pity to mar it by the very slightest touch of artificiality.

ever

G.B.S.

10 *With earnings from* Cyrano, *Loraine was able to pay back some debts to Shaw, including unpaid royalties on a Canadian tour of* Man and Superman *in January 1913 (which Shaw declined).*[21] *American theatrical impresario Charles Frohman (1860–1915) had produced Loraine's American production of* Man and Superman *in 1905 and successfully managed theatres in London as well. Actor-manager Henry Irving (1838–1905), with whom Shaw frequently clashed, first performed Mathias in the melodrama* The Bells *in 1871 and frequently thereafter. Feodor Ivanovich Chaliapin (1873–1938) was a Russian opera singer with an expressive bass voice, much admired by Shaw.*

[ALS] [Loraine 267–68]

Great Southern Hotel
Parnasilla-on-Sea
Kenmare
Co[unty] Kerry

12 July 1919

My dear Loraine

I enclose a formal receipt so that your papers may be in order.

The £600, or whatever it is, is all nonsense. The play did not make the money. Now if your acting had lost it, and I could contend that the money was there for you to make had you been equal to the occasion, I should claim it remorselessly. But the facts, as compared with the runs elsewhere, prove that your acting made more money than the play, and of this surplus I had a very substantial whack. There is consequently no real human reason why I should exploit you and Rostand (or another) for money that the wretched *Superman* never earned. The Statute of Limitations, which has already written off the item legally, is for once right as well as convenient.

All these wonderful Napoleons of finance and business are eminent only because they spend £200 on what their cooks could buy for twopence. Think of poor Charles Frohman, who never owned a theatre or a penny beyond his travelling expenses!

It is too soon to revive *Superman* as a regular production. A revival would be taken as a flag of distress. You must make Tanner a repertory part, like Irving's Mathias in *The Bells*: that is all there is now left in him.

Have you ever considered the fact that Shakespear was *made* by the enormous success of *Henry VI* [?] The public liked the fights and the rapid tragic episodes so much that they stood three plays of it. I have always believed that this success could be repeated. You could make a *novel* sensation with it, and then follow up with *Richard III*.

Without the three plays here under my hand I cannot say exactly how the thing should be done. The first part is very crude; but the death of Beaufort, and the Suffolk-Margaret and Talbot scenes are effective. The second and third parts are much finer: one always remembers York at bay, and "O tyger's heart wrapt in a woman's hide" [*Henry VI, Part* 3, I.iv.,138], which would tax even Chaliapine's [sic] power of crying like a baby.

I suppose the ideal thing would be to get them all on, and play the whole set twice a week. People would *have* to see the three if they saw one. And as the casts are the same people, it would not mean three casts. There would be a tidy bill for armour and silken heraldic coats; but the armour pays its way if the play bites.

Then *Richard* as the grand climax. Somehow, I do not believe in Richard until the ground has been prepared for him by a revival of interest in "histories." *Then* he would go like mad.

I am very doubtful about *Henry V*. People are sick of Jingoism, and fed up with the Agincourt speeches.

We shall be here until the end of August, probably. The tetralogy will keep my holiday busy.

G.B.S.

11 *Loraine did not pursue Shaw's Shakespearean idea, choosing instead to return to familiar Shavian territory with a revival of* Arms and the Man *at the Duke of York's on 11 December 1919, again playing Bluntschli (with Mrs Patrick Campbell as Raina).*[22] *Shaw attended some rehearsals and, true to form, gave Loraine the benefit of his advice.*

After seeing a matinee on 13 December, however, he expressed, in no uncertain terms, his displeasure with the production—and with Loraine in particular. M.R. Morand (1860–1922) played Petkoff, Gerald Lawrence (1873–1957) Sergius, Dorothy Holmes-Gore (1896–1977) Louka, Arthur Whitby (1869–1922) Nicola, and Beverly Sitgreaves (1867–1943) Catherine. The production ran for 72 performances.[23]

[TLS] [Loraine 268–71] [*CL* 3:646–48]

Ayot St Lawrence
Welwyn, Herts.

14 December 1919

My dear Loraine

I went to the matinée yesterday and was horrified to find that the experience of 1894 was repeating itself.[24] On that occasion there was a wildly successful first night, on which the company was anxiously doing its best with the play, and wondering what would happen. What happened was that they were overwhelmed with laughter and applause. This set their minds completely at ease; and at the subsequent performances they played for the laughs and didn't get them. This was the beginning of that detestable effect as of all the characters being so many Shaws spouting Shavianisms, and provoking first a lot of shallow but willing laughter, and then producing disappointment and irritation. That seemed to me to be exactly what was happening yesterday. I did not enjoy myself a bit; and the audience, which came anticipating a great treat, cooled down all through and ended by being annoyed and rather cross. Somebody hissed vigorously; and I felt extremely obliged to him. If it had not been for Morand, who stuck to his part all through, and showed no consciousness of the audience or of his points, I believe the whole audience would have hooted unanimously. Lawrence also acted conscientiously and held the thing together; but he was too mild (I am sending him a line about it) and was a little bothered by Louka, who made orator's gestures like himself, and dug him in the ribs twice in a way horribly out of character. Whitby was all right, because he managed to keep up the dramatic illusion, though he was really fudging his way through the part.

The rest wasn't silence; I wish it had been. No doubt the audience thought your performance fine; but it was quite infamous. You were simply collecting laughs, asking for them, waiting for them, and not pretending to do anything else except once or twice, when you forgot yourself and acted instinctively. The audience was just longing to be allowed to believe in the play, and you wouldn't let it. For a moment, in the waterpipe scene, you looked as if you were going to be slightly drowsy; but after Raina's exit your arch wideawakeness would have roused the Sleeping Beauty. There was not the faintest indication of fatigue or somnolence: at most you seemed without any reason to have become skittishly drunk. The scenes with Raina in this act were breezy beyond description. You worked that attitude with one foot on the dais to death; and the harder you worked it the breezier you became. There was nothing to appeal to the woman or the sympathy of the audience. You were playing her off the stage, a thing no woman likes; and you were defying them to take you seriously.

The third act was not so bad, because it couldn't be. But it was desperately wanting in variety. You were visibly scoring the whole time; and the end of that inevitably is that the score loses it value. You sometimes remind me of a Dublin actor who played Richard III and refused to be beaten by Richmond in the fight. You will not admit that Bluntschli can ever be naive or peppery or anything but victorious, just as you would never admit the tragic defeat of Tanner in *Man & Superman*. You are sometimes like Grummer in *Pickwick* [Dickens' *Pickwick Papers*, 1836]: when a laugh is approaching you have the smile of a favorite: that is how you got the laugh for the machine gun before you mentioned it. It is like

Grouse in the Gun Room.[25] Unluckily, Nature has endowed you with a certain irreduceable [sic] minimum of good acting which saves you from the worst extremities of disaster, and gets praise for you when you are disgracing yourself with every conceivable histrionic profligacy; but you cannot take me in; and, what is more important to both of us just now, you cannot make a success of *Arms & The Man* by such games.

These horrors did not happen when we rehearsed the play in the dead silence which ought to reign in the theatre from the rise of the curtain to its fall. There was illusion, then, even when there was no scenery and no costume. *Cyrano* was listened to in silence. It would not have had a dog'[s] chance if you had had to stop after every line to let the mob heehaw. I have on two occasions tried public appeals for silence with some success. But the only way to compel the audience to take matters into their own hands is to ignore the laughs and go steadily through them, actually trying to make the audience lose as much as possible of the play through their own noisiness. Remember that the lines one does not hear are always the best in the play. And though the words may be lost, the play can at least be seen without any interruption or disillusion. When Raina is seen to open her mouth to speak, and then shut it again and wait quite obviously until the audience has finished butting into Bulgaria, there is an end of the play. A very skilful old hand can sometimes keep up enough action through a laugh (Morand does this) to save the situation; but this is quite beyond Stella at present; and you don't even want to do it, God forgive you.[26] *I* should give orders that the audience was to be absolutely ignored, and that the company must play deafly and blindly in the play and for the play no matter whether they were heard or not. But you like the audience to join in the representation, and invite them to do so. The result will be a failure. In spite of the first night notices the public will soon find that the play is an irritating Shavian bore, with no characters in it and no emotion; and they will stay away. Your eight weeks will become six. Never mind: *I* shall be blamed.

Here are some points of detail.

Louka is too patient at the door whilst you are hiding behind the curtain: she should knock, not violently, but quickly and urgently, between the speeches.

Raina, whilst you are closing the shutters, should take a wrap from the chest of drawers, opening and shutting a drawer to do it, and play the rest of the scene in gold or silver tissue. There is too much of the nighty; and it is not natural that she should not cover up a bit.

She must not forget to ask you what you will do, as the answer about the first man in sounds idiotic without a cue; and she must not forget that the "Oh, THANK you" when you throw her the cloak is a leading point, as it explains the change of feeling that makes her save you. And she must scream out Stop *through* the shots: there is no effect when she waits.

That silly band must not play the Liszt rhapsody as an entr'acte unless you are prepared to let them finish it. They were stopped just as they were beginning the part the audience liked; and the effect was very bad, as if the management knew nothing about music and cared less.

Why did Louka not begin the second act on the chair, hanging out the stockings? The point of that arrangement is that it explains the presence of an otherwise inexplicable and improbable chair where no chair could be in the ordinary course of nature. And it gives a reason for Louka's being in the garden.

Catherine, instead of picking up the act by a bustling entry after the solemn scene between Sergius and Raina, lets it drop. People actually began to cough. Nicola messed the dropping of the bag by not turning his back to the audience and so getting his right hand next [to] Petkoff. Sergius forgot to give his whip to Nicola, and presently found himself in trouble with it.

The third act was half ruined from the start by the absence of Raina when the curtain went up. Not only was the picture spoiled without its apex, but there was a psychological vacancy: Bluntschli without Raina, and Sergius the central figure. Why did you start the act without her?

Stella's inexperience made matters worse. When the Petkoffs go out, it is Raina's business to change the tone and speed and make the requisite pause to announce to the audience that a new scene has begun—the big duet. She picked up the cue "keep discipline for them" and went on at exactly the speed of the previous scene as if she were continuing it; and the result was that you lost half a dozen points before the audience readjusted itself. I told her to say "Please be serious, Captain Bluntschli" after "don't tell him" because it was evident she had not the skills to convey that by her tone in the next sentence. And there again, the audience could not follow her thought; and the scene suffered very much, getting no more effect than a pair of amateurs would have got from barely repeating the lines. And you clung to your Hallo (after my getting you out of it) as if it were the gem of the part.

What is an unfortunate author to do with people who WON'T be helped? The play is one that would get laughs if it were read by schoolchildren. I don't need actors to get those silly laughs: I get them myself. What the actors are for is to produce the illusion that real things are happening to real people, and affecting their feelings. But you are now behaving as if the thing to do was to get the laughs and let everything else go hang. But you see the result. You cannot have mistaken the shallow halfhearted brief throw-a-bone-to-a-dog applause of Saturday afternoon for the real interest which converted even the critics on Thursday to the belief that the play was a play after all. If you will only play with complete sincerity and complete unconsciousness of the audience, and carry out the author's instructions as to the business and the changes of tempo, you will get back Thursday's atmosphere and applause. If you dont, you are in for a dead certain failure; and I will shake the dust of the stage from my feet and refuse to allow any more performances of my plays at all.

Do you think you could inspire Stella to say "to my chocolate cream soldier" a little more feelingly than "to the postman"? I know you think it doesn't matter—that you can do the whole darned thing yourself. But you can't: not even the half of it. If only you will take care of the other parts, they will take care of yours.

I have only one last request. Tell the flashlight man to send me a set of prints (unmounted) and then bill for them.

ever,

G.B.S.

12 *In a slightly more forgiving and constructive mood, Shaw wrote again about* Arms and the Man, *giving detailed insights into how Bluntschli should be acted. Whatever Mrs Campbell's (Stella's) "misfortune" was at the matinee, it did not affect her enjoyment of the production. She wrote to Shaw on 5 January 1919 to say how "delighted" she was with it: "it went splendidly— heavenly chuckles all around me" (Dent 228–29). Mrs Campbell's lodgings in Hogarth Rd (in the Earl's Court district of southwest London) were about 6 km from the Duke of York's Theatre in St Martin's Lane in central London.*

[TLS] [PU]

Ayot St Lawrence
Welwyn, Herts.

20 December 1919

My dear Loraine

I have been struggling to write to you for some days past; but the pressure of other utterly unpostponable matters has prevented me. Meanwhile the returns from *Arms & the Man* are eloquent.

Now I remain convinced that there is at least half as much money again in your Bluntschli; and it must be my fault if it does not materialize. I have been going over that first act to myself as Bluntschli without bothering about the others (as I had to mostly at rehearsal); and I am not sure that I did not set you wrong by making you drop the drama too much when you were left alone with Raina. On thinking it out from the acting point of view, I have arrived at the following conclusions, which you might experiment with on the dog.

First, there should be a very strong contrast between the fugitive Bluntschli and the cheerful well groomed man of the second and third acts. The entry in the garden should not be a reappearance, but a surprise. In the first act he should be, as to his face, like a chimney sweep, haggard under the dirt, and generally in a desperate condition. The contrast with Raina should be extreme.

Second, though it is important that his terror should drop from him—or rather his sense of danger—the moment the narrow shave is over, the effect of this should be to deliver him over to fatigue. "Nothing keeps me awake except danger" is the main clue to the scene. The narrow shave would keep him going fairly well during the "Don't hate me" scene; but when he sits down the first intimation of his dazed sleepiness should come whilst Raina is crossing to the ottoman. This will make his violent start all the more natural. There should be a distinct stroke of facial expression as he takes the pistol from her: a sort of intense weariness behind his grin. Immediately after this the gobbling of the chocolate takes up the thread of his hunger and fatigue; and it is the chocolate that keeps him going through the cavalry charge scene and until "Down that Waterpipe: stop." Then he can pile on the exhaustion for all his is worth, and thus give much more effect to the rise she gets out of him by her exclamation "But what am I to do with you?"

He must not play the "I am a Petkoff" scene brightly. If he does, he kills Raina and kills his whole act. His weariness should be apparent all through. She has to do the brightness, and he should be rueful and forlorn in his efforts to play up to her. And here comes in the question of the attitude. Bluntschli standing with one foot on the dais looks frightfully strong and commanding. He should never look like that except for a moment in the "Do you hear that, you chocolate cream soldier, you?" scene. Instead, he should find all sorts of attitudes and tricks with the bedpost to suggest that he can hardly stand, and that she is unconsciously being cruel to him in her preoccupation with Vienna and Ernani and so forth. The audience must know that the moment she leaves him he will infallibly fall fast asleep. One of my mistakes is the yawning. A man in that condition does not yawn. He may sigh; but yawning indicates a quite natural unexhausted sleepiness. Also, it tends to set the audience yawning, being infectious; for instance, writing these words makes me want to yawn. I believe the yawning business as she goes out can be done just as effectively and much more naturally by letting his head droop as if it were going to drop off.

If the effect of this is to get rid of the laughs, or to get them right (that is, to soften them until it is possible to play through them) so much the better. The laughs are not drawing money: they are keeping it out of the house. There were no laughs in *Cyrano*; and what people miss in Bluntschli is Cyrano's nose: they want the pathos, the defeat, that underlay Cyrano from beginning to end. Now Bluntschli is not a tragic figure, and is not defeated; but it does not follow that Loraine as Bluntschli cannot make the appeal of Loraine as Cyrano. It can only come in the first act, because in the second comes on the tragic and defeated Sergius, who is now getting all the sympathy of the reaction after the war. But Bluntschli has the start for a whole act, which is quite enough to establish him as a sympathetic figure, who is not callous merely because he has never been in trouble. Just think it over and try experiments. Besides, as the part will be a permanent repertory one with you, it is worth while to work it up elaborately.

I had to hold hard about interfering until I saw whether the brilliant farce treatment would pay or not. It *might* have. But now it is clear that it does not; so we can both let ourselves rip in getting the performance on to a higher plane of comedy.

Stella will not during this run be able to get an address any nearer to Slivnitza than Hogarth Road; but I believe your shoulders are broad enough to carry her through. It *must* be possible to recapture the first night effect and improve on it. She wrote to me explaining her misfortune in the matinée.

I am down here until the New Year.

ever

G.B.S.

13 *During the run of* Arms and the Man, *Shaw became involved in discussions with Viola Tree (1884–1938) and Mrs Campbell about a* Pygmalion *revival. (Tree's father, Herbert Beerbohm Tree, had created the role of Henry Higgins in the premiere of* Pygmalion *at His Majesty's Theatre in 1914, opposite Mrs Campbell as Eliza.) Shaw was ambivalent about the whole thing, but the revival went ahead—without Loraine—at the Aldwych Theatre on 10 February 1920, with the now 55-year-old Mrs Campbell as Eliza and C. Aubrey Smith (1863–1948) as Higgins. In one letter to Shaw about the shambolic casting and rehearsals for the play, Mrs Campbell described Viola Tree as "a spoilt child playing with dolls, [who] gives every reason for her* *whims except an artistic or business reason" (Dent 232). The production closed on 17 April 1920 after 78 performances.*

[ALS] [PU]

10 Adelphi Terrace
London W.C.2

16 January 1920

My dear Loraine

I am in a horrid mess. Viola Tree wants to revive *Pygmalion* at the Aldwych, with Mrs Campbell. Will you come to lunch tomorrow at 1.30 and let me tell you the difficulties I cannot write. Anyhow, I doubt if the project is possible as it stands. Do you see yourself managed by the Infant Roscius? Even less can I see Mrs Campbell managed by Viola.

Higgins—a mere detail to which Mrs Campbell attaches little importance—looms larger in my view. Charlotte declares you are the only possible Higgins. As *Arms & the Man* won't pay its way, why not change the daughter for the mother and put up *Pygmalion*? I do not recommend this course: I am simply in a hole, and want to get out of it somehow. You are accustomed to barrages.

Ring up my secretary as early as you are afoot—Gerrard 331—and say whether we may expect you.

ever

G.B.S.

14 *As a result of this "truly startling letter," in which Shaw accuses Loraine of acting under the influence of morphia (morphine), Winifred Loraine said that relations between Shaw and Loraine were "really impaired." Shaw claimed it was merely "an irritation," that was "soon forgotten." "But there was," he conceded, "a rift, not an unfriendly one, but a breach which proved permanent." According to Mrs Loraine, it was "highly unlikely" that her husband was under the influence of morphia, which, she says, "always produced in him an uncomfortable feeling of distention" (Loraine 271–74).*

*The Alhambra Music Hall, located in Leicester Square, seated an audience of 3,500. The Shaws expected to see a Tarzan movie there (*Tarzan of the Apes, *1918), but were disappointed. Shaw saw Italian actress Eleonora Duse in Hermann Sudermann's* Magna *at Drury Lane in 1895 (Dukore 2:369–70). The next London revival of* You Never Can Tell *was not until September 1920 (at the Everyman Theatre).*

[TLS] [Loraine 272–73] [*CL* 3:651–53]

10 Adelphi Terrace,
[London] W.C.2

19 January 1920

My dear Loraine

Forgive me, but I wanted to rouse your attention rather violently.

My visit to the play was quite unpremeditated. You told Charlotte that there were lions & tigers in Tarzan; and we went to the Alhambra only to find that it was off. Being stranded, we took refuge in the Duke of York's.

If I were a vain author I should have concluded that you were intoxicated with my comedy. And if I had thought that you had merely been dining, I should not have dreamt of alluding to it. But there was something in your brilliancy that alarmed me. Twenty years ago it would have been natural; and you would not have miscalculated a single stroke. But it was not quite natural: it was just a little miraculous; and once or twice you put the pitch up a shade higher than you meant to. So I thought I would draw you on the subject.

And now here is what I want to know, straight between the eyes. Was it morphia? I know you keep up appearances extraordinarily well; but I also know that if a man gets birds[27] to sing in his flat and has nobody but members of his own profession to talk to (I avoid literary people like the plague) he is lonely; and if he has had his knee shot to pieces he cannot get about without hurting himself more or less. If, in addition, two battle wounds have taught him the virtues of morphia, then, if I see him in a condition of superhuman brilliancy, can you blame me if I wish my eyes were sharp enough to see whether his pupils are quite normal? There! Now the murder is out. If I am, as you say, making a fool of myself, so much the better. But I thought I'd risk it. You see, if it were so, nobody else would tell you, because it would be an offensive thing to mention, and no business of theirs anyhow. Besides, they think that everyone who touches morphia for a minute is a morphinomaniac.

I once saw Duse play Magda under the influence of a dose of morphia after seeing her play it quite naturally a few nights before. It gave the same brilliant effect; but it was not quite right; and the effect on the audience was nothing like as great.

By the way, what is so very exasperating about me in spite of my amiable qualities, is not that I am an egotistical and ridiculous author. Consider it a moment, and you will admit that an author's vanity would make you laugh quite goodhumouredly. What infuriates people is my incorrigible habit of constituting myself, uninvited, their solicitor, their doctor, and their spiritual director without the smallest delicacy. I have no right whatever to concern myself with your personal habits or your private welfare; but you see I do. I treat everyone sympathetically as an invalid, injudicious in diet, politically foolish, probably intemperate, more or less mendacious and dishonest; and, however friendly my disposition and cheerful my way of putting it, they don't like it. I can't help it. After all, you cannot reasonably expect a playwright to mind his own business. Other people are his business. And his infernal meddlesomeness is sometimes useful. So be as charitable as you can.

Now somebody wants to revive *You Never Can Tell.*

ever

G.B.S.

15 *After* Arms and the Man *closed in February 1920, Loraine vacationed in Europe (and, for a few days, was feared dead after the plane he was piloting disappeared over the Alps) before returning to the West End in J.M. Barrie's new play* Mary Rose, *which opened at the Haymarket on 22 April 1920 and ran for just one short of four hundred performances. Loraine, however, tired and debilitated by his war wounds, left the production well before the end of the run, and embarked on a world cruise, on which he met his future wife (and biographer) Winifred Strangman (they married in London on 14 July 1921—on borrowed money). West End offers dried up until Loraine appeared in Harley Granville Barker's* *adaptation of Sacha Guitry's (1885–1957) comedy* Deburau, *which closed, however, after only 28 performances at the Ambassadors Theatre in November 1921. Loraine had also started exploring possibilities in film, leading in 1922 to his first film appearance, in a silent movie called* Bentley's Conscience. *The "big job" that Shaw had completed by early 1922 was the acting script of* Back to Methuselah *for its world premiere by the Theatre Guild at the Garrick Theatre in New York, where Parts I and II opened on 27 February. The Guild, founded by Lawrence Langner (1890–1962) in 1919, had already presented the world premiere of* Heartbreak House *in 1920 and would soon (December 1923) also mount the world premiere of* Saint Joan. *Vaughan Thomas was the Guild's London agent. The Guild's production of* The Devil's Disciple *opened at the Garrick Theatre in New York on 23 April 1923 and ran for 64 performances. Langner had initially proposed to use one of two "Huns" in the cast (as Dudgeon), either (Vienna-born) Joseph Schildkraut (1862–1930) or Frank Reicher (1875–1965) (Langner 84), but neither made the final cut. Shaw's concern was the political sensitivity of having a German lead in a high profile production about a US–UK war while a major post-war international disarmament conference was being held in Washington (12 November 1921 to 6 February 1922). "If I accepted Schildkraut or Reicher . . . the play would be produced three weeks from now with a German hero, the theatre burnt, and the directors lynched," he told Guild designer Lee Simonson (*CL *3:751, 11 November 1921).*

Shaw owned several cars after acquiring his first, manufactured by the French company Lorraine-Dietrich, in 1908. Hatfield railway station is about 12 km south of Ayot St Lawrence.

[ALS] [PU]

Ayot St Lawrence
Welwyn, Herts.

8 January 1922

My dear Loraine

We have been down here continuously for many weeks, I with a big job on my hands which prevented me from attending to anything else. Now that it is finished I realize that the Theatre Guild and Vaughan Thomas have been making despairing appeals to me to settle about the *D's D*. Have you any views? I cannot, after all that has passed, hold them up much longer, as they have made the scenery. Only they *will* keep proposing either quite impossible people or else Huns; and though France is doing her best to drive us into a German alliance, it may not come off in time. Is there money enough in the film business to keep you on this side?

Deburau was damnable: that was why it was damned. All very well for Guitry, who is nothing if not elderly, and needs plays in which the strong scenes are the elderly ones, but quite inopportune for you. To hear you giving the worst possible advice to a lumping son of 22, and congratulating him on his consequent ruinous exhibition of incompetence was really very trying. What a crew they were! Of course you did the garret scene on your head; but so much the worse: it was a darned sight too convincing: you acted 20 years on to your age.

Are you film-free to the extent of coming down here to lunch some day; or would it bore you? Monday or Tuesday, the 16th & 17th, would suit us. In that case would you come in your car; or shall I pick you up at Hatfield? I have a new little car; but if I use that I shall have to shove you into the dicky and entertain

Mrs Loraine inside whilst I drive. The coupé barely holds two: Charlotte and I nearly burst it. If it be wet,¦ I can bring the old Lorraine-Dietrich.

Ever

G.B.S.

16 *Arthur Wing Pinero's (1855–1934)* The Second Mrs Tanqueray, *with Gladys Cooper (1888–1971) as Paula Tanqueray, was revived at the Playhouse Theatre on 3 June 1922, and ran for 220 performances. (By way of contrast, Loraine was acting at the time of Shaw's letter at the Duke of York's in a forgettable comedy by Monckton Hoffe called* Pomp and Circumstance, *which lasted for just 18 performances.) As always, Loraine was contemplating a revival of* Man and Superman, *but other than Gladys Cooper, Shaw could not think of a suitable Ann Whitefield, except perhaps Phyllis Neilson-Terry (1892–1977), niece of Ellen Terry (1847–1928). Lawrence Langner expected the Theatre Guild's 1922 production of* Back to Methuselah *to lose $30,000 (£6,000); he never expected it to break even (wishful thinking on Shaw's part), and was relieved when the loss came in at only $20,000 (£4,000) (Langner 51–52). To subsidize plays such as* Methuselah *and* Heartbreak House, *the Guild needed popular successes such as Ferenc Molnár's* Liliom, *which ran for three hundred performances in New York between April 1921 and January 1922, the cast headed by Joseph Schildkraut (see letter #15). Neither Schildkraut nor John Barrymore (1882–1942) nor Frank Reicher (see letter #15) appeared in* The Devil's Disciple *or* Caesar and Cleopatra *(Guild Theatre, New York, 13 April 1925).*

Malvern, a spa town in Worcestershire, was a holiday destination for the Shaws. In 1929, Barry Jackson (1879–1961) founded a summer repertory theatre there with the express purpose of producing Shaw's plays. The poster Shaw saw in Malvern refers to Loraine's film Bentley's Conscience *(see letter #15).*

[ALS] [PU]

Ayot St Lawrence
Welwyn, Herts.

18 June 1922

[No salutation]

I hear that *Tanqueray* is playing to full houses. This will set a fashion for New Women in Old Plays. Why not G.C. for Anne [sic]? There is nothing else on the cards except Phyllis N.T.; and the Ts are not Anne's sort.

 I have had to let the *D's D.* go for America. The Theatre Guild calculated on losing £6000 by *Methuselah*, but considered the honor & glory worth it. They did not lose that: in fact Langner believes they broke even (I shall get precise details through him presently); but they can indulge in these ventures only by exploiting a popular success occasionally. Schildkraut as Liliom was the real backing of *Heartbreak House* and *Methuselah*; and they want to try out Schildkraut or Barrymore in the *D's D.* to support a revival of *Caesar & Cleopatra* with Reicher. I could not with any sort of moral reasonableness fence with them any longer about it; so I told them to go ahead.

 When we went to Malvern for Easter we just missed a strikingly billed

First Appearance of Famous Airman-Actor in Bentley

Fate drives you to the Legitimate: old or new. Those silly potboilers that don't even boil the pot are too disappointing for anything. If you do any more of them I will write a play for you and call it

The Hoodoo.

Better starve as The Who Doesn't. Tuesday, then, at 4.

G.B.S.

17 *With nothing in the offing since the* Pomp and Circumstance *flop (letter #16), Loraine was still agitating for a remounting of* Man and Superman. *But far better, Shaw now advised, to seek a new play, such as Somerset Maugham's* East of Suez, *which was destined for a good run (209 performances) at His Majesty's when it opened on 2 September 1922—but sans Loraine. Moreover, it seems that Loraine's overtures to Gladys Cooper to join him (as Ann Whitefield) in* Man and Superman *were unsuccessful anyway, so, for now at least, he dropped the idea. The small Everyman Theatre (now a cinema), in the Hampstead area of London, opened in 1920, and in 1921 it became the first London theatre to mount a repertory season of Shaw plays. It was a far less expensive theatre to rent than those in the West End, but paid lower salaries to actors. Shaw's "destination not yet settled" was the seaside town of Tenby in Pembrokeshire, southwest Wales. Shaw's communication with his bank was probably related to Loraine paying back a debt. He had loaned Loraine £600 in January 1922 (BL Add MS 50518 f 297). In a brief letter to Loraine dated 23 March 1923 (Grapes), Shaw acknowledged that "the bank has sent me the bond," and that "the transaction has cost me absolutely nothing."*

[ALS] [PU]

Walton Park Hotel
Clevedon
Somerset

18 July 1922

My dear Loraine

All the better. The Superman has an ancient and fishlike smell by this time [like Caliban in *The Tempest*, II.ii]; and *East of Suez* is fire-new from a younger mint. In the West End it is better to be the indispensable man in the latest thing: starring in masterpieces is provincial, and should be kept for the provinces, where the human soul still lingers.

I am convinced that when *M&S* is old enough to be received like *Mrs Tanqueray*, it will revive as a woman's play. It needs a new woman and a young woman, as Lillah [McCarthy] was in 1904. Tanner probably needs a new and young man; but as an incompetent will kill the play, and there is a personal specialization in your case which is not for an age but for all time, nobody else is in the running.

It is quite natural that if G.C. is on the crest of her wave with *Mrs T* she should not be much interested in Ann. It always needs a period of prolonged and acute starvation to reduce West End favorites to Shavianism. Then they go to the Everyman for £3 a week and share in the commonwealth.

We shall leave this place, which resembles the south side of the Thames between Hungerford & Waterloo bridges at low water, on Saturday next, the 23rd, for some destination not yet settled.

I have written to the bank.

Ever

G. Bernard Shaw

18 *What was enclosed with this letter is unknown. It seems that Shaw was ready to hold* The Devil's Disciple *for Loraine (as Burgoyne), but under pressure from would-be director of the play Lewis Casson (1875–1969) the commitment was qualified. Russell Thorndike (1885–1972), brother of the more famous Sybil Thorndike (1882–1976, wife of Lewis Casson), achieved the unusual distinction, at the age of 37, of playing both Lear and Hamlet in the space of a few weeks in March and April 1922 at the Old Vic. The Ambassadors Theatre had a seating capacity of five hundred, and in addition to the small size of the theatre it seems that Shaw's political sensitivities about* The Devil's Disciple *extended to London as well as New York (see letter #15). Loraine had turned down an offer of a role in Somerset Maugham's* East of Suez *(see letter #17). Godalming is a town in Surrey, about 70 km southwest of central London. Shaw had been a member of the Fabian Society since 1884 and regularly participated in its summer schools in Godalming and elsewhere.*

[ALS] [PU]

Hotel
Co[unty] Wexford
Rosslare
Ireland

17 August 1922

My dear Loraine

Look at the enclosed (I don't want it back).

I don't think the Ambassadors big enough for the play; and I don't think the political moment propitious for it; but I *do* think that Thorndike is a possible Dick.

Although it is almost impossible to refuse a play to a competent actor on the ground that it is being held up for another actor, I have told Casson that you have the refusal of the play for the moment, and that I had rather leave the matter open for a while. I have also put to him the objection to the theatre and to the political atmosphere.

But if Thorndike sticks to it hard, and offers a bigger theatre, he will be able to ask me, if I refuse, whether I am genuinely in business, or only using my plays to gratify my personal partialities. Probably his own views are too personal to allow him to think of playing that card; but he would have it in his hand all the same.

What are your prospects when you have passed *Suez*? Or shall I say yes if he can secure you for Burgoyne? Or what the devil shall I do?

I return to England on Sunday, leaving Charlotte behind in Dublin. My address until the 30th will be Fabian Summer School, Priors Field, Godalming.

Ever

G.B.S.

19 *Loraine's search for a play that would give him a long West End run led to a role in a comedy by Ian Hay (pseudonym for John Hay Beith, 1876–1952) called* The Happy Ending, *which opened at the St James's Theatre on 30 November 1922, but lasted for only a disappointing 43 performances.*[28] *Not surprisingly, then, and despite Shaw's previous objections, Loraine was still hankering after a revival of* Man and Superman. *In his productions of the play in America he had made it, Shaw suggests, "unisexual" by overshadowing actresses playing Ann, but in the British premiere at the Court Theatre in 1905 Lillah McCarthy had made sure that Ann was Tanner's equal. And that's the way Shaw liked it, although students from Vassar, a private women's college (coeducational since 1969) about 150 km north of New York, seem to* *have been entirely happy with Loraine's dominant performance. Faith Calli (1888–1942) played Miss Eynsford-Hill in Viola Tree's 1920 revival of* Pygmalion *(see letter #13). The "Hoares" in the opening sentence and Mrs Loraine's "diamond man" in the last have not been identified, though in the first instance Shaw may have been referring to playwright Douglas Hoare, whose plays and adaptations were frequently performed in the 1910s and 1920s.*

[ALS] [PU]

10 Adelphi Terrace
London, W.C.2

16 January 1923

My dear Loraine

I have written to the Hoares to renew.

As to Tanner I should not mind your ripening years so much if the play were a little less decrepit. It might revive like *Tanqueray* if we could find a new first class Vamp to play Ann, but ten Tanners cannot pull it through without a heroine. Male and female created I them; and though you succeeded in making the play unisexual in America, where the contrary tradition had not been established, and when you were so young and beautiful that all Vassar came night after night to New York to hear you, it was no use in London, where Lillah had been beforehand with you. Anyhow, it is not possible to establish a management without a strong leading lady, especially when you have compromised yourself as an actor psychologically by going through two wars as a real person. You didn't act *The Happy Ending*: you held it up to derision. You have broken out of the enchanted palace; and only the toughest parts and the toughest plays will bear your touch without withering.

My only cert so far is *Pygmalion*: another woman's job; but it has been revived already; only it should have been with you and Faith Calli.

Will you beg Mrs Loraine to write the name and address of her diamond man on the enclosed card & post it to me. I have mislaid the note I made of it: it was Hyslop, I think, but if so he is not in the telephone book.

ever

G.B.S.

20 *In the early 1920s Loraine's career continued apace in London, mostly mundanely, but with occasional bright spots, one of which was a sparkling performance as Mirabell in Congreve's comedy* The Way of the World, *opposite Edith Evans as Millamant, at the Lyric Theatre, Hammersmith, in 1924 (158 performances). In September 1924 Loraine returned to the United States to reprise his London success at the Garrick in a play called* Tiger Cats *(by "Michael Orme" [Mrs J.T. Grein]). Katharine Cornell was in the American cast. Later that year Loraine announced a Shaw season in New York, but was warned off it by Shaw because American rights to his plays (including* Man and Superman*) were now owned by the Theatre Guild (Grapes, 29 December 1924 and 2[?] February 1925). Back and forth across the Atlantic, Loraine was finding it increasingly difficult to get major roles. "Why don't you go into parliament and chuck the wretched stage?" Shaw asked (Grapes, [2?] February 1925). But Loraine held on, and, when all else failed, reverted once more to* Arms and the Man *for a short run at the Everyman in September 1926. The Everyman hoped for a transfer to the West End, but Shaw resisted: "Any West End manager with an atom of sense," he told Loraine, "can come straight to me or to you and* *get a clean deal without any third party claims" (Grapes, 4 September 1926). Shaw in the meantime was on holiday in Italy, having recovered from a bout of influenza in March 1926, which he linked to a fall in Ireland in September 1923 (i.e., three, not two, years previously).* Captain Brassbound's Conversion *was not revived until November 1929, when it had a short run at the Everyman, with Shirley Bax as Lady Cicely. Loraine never played Brassbound, and Mrs Campbell never played Lady Cicely. Shaw's colourful criticism of Mrs Campbell in this letter is a recurring feature of his stormy relationship with her over many years. He calls upon Falstaff's appeal to Hal in II.iv of* Henry IV Part I *to warn Loraine off Mrs Campbell.*

[ALS] [PU]

Regina Palace Hotel
Stresa
Lago Maggiore
Italy

16 September 1926

My dear Loraine

My communication was provoked by a series of messages from the Everyman, all peremptorily demanding replies by wire, and assurances that I would not object to a transfer to the West End, and so on and so forth, which suggested that the managers might have told you that they held the play. They seemed to think so themselves. So I thought there would be no harm in dropping you a line, especially as it is so long since we have waved a hand to one another. I have heard from you occasionally all over the place, or rather all over the Atlantic; and I am only just quit of a serious illness that felled me in March, a sequel, I suspect, to an accident in Ireland two years ago.

You could, of course, play Brassbound on your head; but Stella couldn't and wouldn't play Lady Cicely, though she would jump at an appearance in the part. She would explain to you that there is something hopelessly wrong with your person, and that you are no gentleman; and she would stop the rehearsals every ten seconds to shew you what you were to do next. She would insult all the poorer members of the cast. In short, she would drive you and everyone else raving mad. There was a time when even in a ruined play she could attract an audience by her personal fascination; but that time is past, I presume (on the calendar: I havn't seen her play lately).

Nothing but actual hair blanching experience could give you a notion of what she is professionally. In spite of her wonderful art of exploiting her charm, and the unerring rightness of her intonation, she has never learnt her legitimate business, and won't be taught it. She is helpless without a producer, and yet never stops telling everyone what to do (especially *after* they have done it), and pushing the furniture up the stage, as she cannot use the front. Her sole notion of lighting is a spot lime in the glare of which her face flattens out into a white plate with two plums on it, and her figure looks like nothing at all. Her genius for disconcerting and discouraging everyone who tries to act with her is amazing. Off the stage she can be irresistible when she wants to; but professionally a single experience is enough to finish her most devoted admirer. She would age you by [a] quarter of a century in a fortnight, and might quite possibly kill you. So no more of that, Hal, an thou lov'st me.

West End management, except on very favorable sharing terms, is, as you say, impossible. Until a lot of new theatres which will hold three or four thousand pounds at low prices are built, the situation will remain precarious.

ever

G.B.S.

21 *The Shaws did not get back from Italy in time to see Loraine in* Arms and the Man *at the Everyman. Lucie Evelyn ("L.E.") didn't fulfil her ambition to play Eliza, but she did later appear in Part IV of* Back to Methuselah *(in March 1928 at the Court as Mrs Badger-Bluebin; Ralph Richardson played Zozim). Alma Murray (1854?–1945) created the role of Raina in the original production of* Arms and the Man *at the Avenue Theatre on 21 April 1894. Jeanne de Casalis ("Miss de C.") (1897–1966) appeared as the Strange Lady in* The Man of Destiny *at the Everyman in June 1924. Despite Shaw's imploring, Loraine never played Sergius. The "lady at Hampstead" (i.e., the Everyman) who played Louka was Joyce Kennedy (1898?–1943). Gerald du Maurier (1873–1934) never played Bluntschli, and Gladys Cooper (see letter #17) never played Raina.*

[TLS] [PU]

10 Adelphi Terrace
London W.C.2

9 October 1926

My dear Loraine

We arrived on Tuesday, just too late for the Everyman. Your name and portrait produced quite a good lot of paragraphs: in fact you were all over the papers, unless my press cuttings were forged.

L.E. wants to play *Pygmalion*. But these casts of matrons, skilful and experienced as they are, lack something that the playgoer needs. I have never seen L.E., and so write without prejudice; but the crushing experience of the results of faithfulness to old favorites compels me to put an age limit to Raina. Otherwise I should have to give the part to Alma Murray, the original and the best.

Miss de C. should have done well enough: her Strange Lady in *The Man of Destiny* was quite good; but you never can tell. I am afraid the play is worn out as a Bluntschli attraction. Nobody can play Bluntschli better than you; but then anybody can play him well enough and get away with it. Why don't you play Sergius, a part which has never been really played yet for all it is worth? With a good Louka (and the lady at Hampstead got very fine notices) the pair would become the heavy centre of the piece, with Bluntschli and Raina as comic relief. If you could induce du Maurier to play B. to your S., with Gladys Cooper as Raina, there would be a really promising west end revival in it. But for all cheaper purposes the piece is played out. The one thing you can't do with the part is to rouse the smallest curiosity as to how you will play it. Think of the curiosity about Gerald as B. and you as S!

Think it over.

Ever

G.B.S.

22 *Loraine remained in the theatrical doldrums for the next two years, doing the odd Shakespeare matinee or two, doodling a film script about his war experiences, and falling into depression. Then he discovered Strindberg. With Loraine in the title role,* The Father *opened at the Everyman on 3 August 1927 (in a double bill with Shaw's* Overruled, *but not with Loraine in that cast), followed by a transfer to the Savoy and then the Apollo in the West End. Immediately after* The Father *closed (29 October 1927), Loraine took over the lease of the Apollo for an indefinite period. His second Strindberg,* The Dance of Death, *with Loraine as Edgar, opened there on 16 January 1928. Neither of the Strindbergs achieved a long run (92 and*

40 performances, respectively), but they restored Loraine's self-esteem. A revival of Cyrano de Bergerac *at the Apollo in November 1927, with Winifred Loraine as Roxane (and costume designer), however, managed only 37 performances. Shaw missed all three productions but was aware of disagreements between Loraine and Baron Erik Kule Palmstierna, the Swedish Ambassador to the United Kingdom, over the translation of* The Dance of Death. *Shaw's encouragement to Loraine to revive* The Dance of Death *in a new translation, funded by the Anglo-Swedish Literary Foundation, was not taken up. Shaw had set up the Foundation—which is still active—with the prize money for the 1925 Nobel Prize for Literature, which he was awarded in November 1926. The Unknown Warrior, translated by Cecil Lewis from the French (*Le Tombeau sous L'Arc de Triomphe, *by Paul Raynal) opened at the Arts Theatre on 5 February 1928. Even if Loraine saw the play, he showed no further interest in it. What theatre manager and Shaw champion Charles Macdona (1860–1946), had told Shaw about Loraine planning to go to Australia was true. Negotiations took place for Loraine to do* Man and Superman *and* Arms and the Man *there, as part of a Macdona-managed Shaw repertoire, but nothing came of them. The Shaws had moved from Adelphi Terrace to Whitehall Court in July 1927.*

[TLS] [PU]

Ayot St Lawrence
Welwyn, Herts.

19 February 1928

My dear Loraine

A long string of contretemps of one sort or another, including an illness which kept Charlotte in bed for a fortnight (she's all right now) prevented me from seeing three things which I had marked down for a visit: to wit, Winnie (if she will allow me to call her so) in *Cyrano*, supported by Mr Loraine and a London company, and the two Strindbergs. I am a Strindberg fan, and a patron of Swedish literature to the extent of my Nobel prize money, which furnishes your foe Palmstierna (my noble pal) with his war chest. Your telegram was my first intimation that the *Dance* was coming off; and then it was impossible for me to jump in on the last night. But you must bury the hatchet with the Baron (*not* in his skull) and revive the play; for it is worth your while to become a specialist in Strindberg. I gathered from him that you had interpolated two or three acts and an epilogue of your own into the English version; and knowing you to be quite capable of it I did not question his grievance. The American versions are very poor; and the Baron can easily obtain a competent and faithful translation by engaging a translator at the expense of the Anglo-Swedish Foundation whenever you require one. Of course he cannot himself make a translation; and as you presumably know no more Swedish than I, neither can you. Tell him that if he brings you presentable translations which are speakable on the stage, and will guarantee their faithfulness (not to say a fortnight's business) you will play them for him without changing a comma until he is black in the face at the expense of the Swedish Government and the A-S Foundation. I am assured that there are some big historical plays which are first rate star business.

See *The Unknown Warrior* if you can, or indeed whether you can or not. You must not miss it. It has the enormous advantage over *Cyrano* of a salary list of three persons and one scene. It is the sort of play that takes a war to make. The French couldn't stand it at the Théâtre Français.

Is it true that you are going to Australia? Macdona, who has secured all my old plays for that benighted land, told me so.

We have left the Adelphi, and are seldom in London more than two days in the week, which accounts for my apparent remoteness and seclusion.

ever

G.B.S.

23 *Barry Jackson ("B.J.") (see letter #16) was preparing to produce the English premiere of* The Apple Cart *at the Malvern Festival for 19 August 1929. Loraine wanted to do* Arms and the Man *at the Apollo, but Jackson was planning a transfer of* The Apple Cart *from Malvern to the West End (where it opened on 17 September 1929 at the Queen's for a run of 285 performances). Shaw did not think it a good idea to have his new play competing against the popular earlier play (see Shaw's letters to Jackson on the subject, Conolly 44–45). Loraine was not having a happy time at the Apollo Theatre. Shaw wrote this letter on the day that Edwin Burke's comedy,* This Thing Called Love, *starring Loraine, closed after just 32 performances. Loraine then took Shaw's advice to let the theatre. A modern-dress production of* The Merry Wives of Windsor, *headed by Oscar Asche (1871–1936), transferred there from the Haymarket a week after* This Thing Called Love *closed. After Malvern,* The Apple Cart *opened at the Queen's Theatre, managed by Alfred Butt (1878–1962), on 17 September 1929 for a run of 285 performances.*

[ALS] [Loraine 364]

Ayot St Lawrence
Welwyn, Herts.

20 July 1929

My dear Loraine

If you have not already done so, don't approach B.J., as he would be a perfect lunatic if he consented. So would I.

What is the matter at the Apollo is the heat, which would equally affect *Arms*, and the fact that the part, though it begins well, weakens and lapses into convention at the end. After Shaw & Rostand & Strindberg people won't stand tomfooling from you unless it is so good and so well kept up that you can laugh them into being pleased right to the end. That was the real reason why Charlotte wouldn't come round and pretend to like it, though of course she pleads her very sound rule that dressingroom visits are horrible nuisances when people are undressing and getting off their make-up, and that the business of any audience is to go home to bed.

Anyhow, what on earth is the use of producing a play at the end of July with the thermometer at 90° in the shade? *Let* the theatre: there are always idiots who will take it for the dog days.

As to Butt, it will be either the Globe or the Queen's: the contract is concluded.

ever

G.B.S.

24 *After plans for Australia were dropped, and after giving up the Apollo (with debts of £7,000), Loraine continued criss-crossing the Atlantic in search of work, still beset by financial difficulties, to which were added a failing marriage and ill-health (leading to the "surgical procedures" referred to by Shaw, which took place in Chicago in June 1932 [Liggera 214]). So yet again Loraine turned to Shaw for succour. It was another American revival of* Man and Superman. *Shaw approved a short run in Newport, Rhode Island, in July 1932, and then (unsuccessfully) sought the Theatre Guild's support for a New York production of the full-length play. No other management, including the Shubert Organization, filled the breach, and the Guild never did produce* Man and Superman *(though Loraine did appear in non-Shavian Guild productions—Thornton Wilder's* Lucrece *in 1932 and Eugene O'Neill's* Days Without End *in 1934, for example). Alfred Lunt (1892–1977) and his wife Lynn Fontanne (1887–1983) were leading (and influential) actors with the Guild. The de Dion was a French-designed car that Loraine had used in his 1905 New York production of* Man and Superman. *As a teenager, on one of his many visits to Dublin theatres, Shaw probably saw English actor Charles Mathews (1803–78) perform in a touring production in the 1870s.*

[ALS] [PU]

4 Whitehall Court
London S.W.1

17 September 1932

[No salutation]

I have just cabled the Guild "Please consider Loraine's *Superman* project seriously[.] [T]he entirety has proved so irresistibly and most unexpectedly attractive here that it strongly suggests a revival with this feature of which Robert alone seems capable."

The Guild is, I guess, really controlled by Lunt and Mrs Lunt (Fontanne); but this stuff in its entirety is too heavy for their taste and possibly for their capacity. And yet she ought not to let Anne [sic] slip by her.

The Guild has done so much for me that I cannot very well deny them the refusal of any revival; but if they will not undertake the entirety themselves they must let Shubert (or another: I thought he was bankrupt) try it.

But are you well advised to attempt the entirety nightly? It is a heavier job than the Hamlet entirety, and will certainly kill you if you do not resolutely bar matinées, and probably kill you anyhow. So for Heaven's sake be careful. Why not a Sunday series? Once a week is enough for any actor. SPEND SUNDAY WITH SHAW would be a good alliterative slogan.

I doubt if costumes of 1902 are worth the bother. Unless they make the women more attractive they will be a handicap. And it would be much easier to adapt the dialogue to the latest supercharged racing car than to yank a de Dion out of a museum.

Besides, why harp on the age of the play? A 30 year old play by an actor of 56 (damn it: you're only 20 years younger than I am) is not exactly a bait for the youth of America, who know nothing about us or about the play, but will take it on its merits, and not as "staging a come back" if you let them alone. You should rather stress your First Appearance in America as Don Juan.

Modernity is the note.

I shudder at your surgical experiences; but if they have slimmed off your Petkoffian waistcoat you may yet rival Charles Mathews, who was over 70 when I saw him play airy juveniles quite plausibly.

But, I repeat, the entirety is a killing job. *Do* be careful.

G.B.S.

25 *In December 1932 the Shaws began a world cruise on the Canadian Pacific liner the* Empress of Britain. *They arrived in San Francisco on 24 March 1933 and were guests at the San Simeon ranch of media baron William Randolph Hearst (1863–1951). They also visited the MGM studios in Culver City—where Shaw met Broadway and Hollywood star Ann Harding (1902–81)—before sailing, via the Panama Canal, to New York, where they arrived on 11 April 1933. Shaw gave a long and controversial talk that night to an audience of 3,500 at the Metropolitan Opera House on "The Future of Political Science in America" (published by Constable in 1933 as* The Political Madhouse in America and Nearer Home*). Next morning he had a crowded breakfast meeting with Loraine—the last time they met—and others (while Charlotte had a quieter time with Armina Marshall [1895–1991], wife of Theatre Guild founder Lawrence Langner and a senior administrator of the Guild), before sailing across a stormy Atlantic ocean for England.*

[ALS] [PU]

Empress of Britain at sea and pitching violently

14 April 1933
Good Friday

My dear Loraine

Just a line to say that I was considerably disappointed at being forced to spoil our breakfast, which ought to have been tête à tête, by the impossibility of crowding the others in in any other way.[29] It was, as you saw, a hellish corobbery [sic]. I have been trying to sleep it off ever since, and am not yet quite myself. All yesterday my head was aching; my teeth were aching; and my kidneys were going mad. Do not take a trip round the globe if you want a rest cure.

I remain ignorant of whether you are coming back or making America your last asylum. Your figure leaves nothing to be desired: evidently your Petkoff period is past and you can go on playing Tanner and Bluntschli until they kill you. And your pep seems undiminished.

I missed Hollywood and saw only Culver City, where Hearst reigns over Metro-Goldwyn-Mayer. I looked into a studio or two, and made Ann Harding laugh; but her press agent thought it would be better publicity if I made her cry, and reported accordingly.

The photography is beautiful: it leaves the British work nowhere. But the stuff they waste it on is pitiful: five sixths of it opening doors and going up and downstairs and the other sixth socking jaws and looking through bedroom keyholes and kissing at great length. And though they know a little of the X.Y.Z. of production in this line, they don't know the A.B.C. of it, and have no notion of what screening a good play involves.

Charlotte apologizes for having had to spend the morning in bed. I smuggled Mrs Langner in; but she saw nobody else.

ever

G. Bernard Shaw

After his final meeting with Shaw, Loraine divided his time between New York and Hollywood (where he made three films in 1934) before returning to England in November 1935. There was just time to pay off some debts and for his wife to divorce him, before he checked into a London hospital with a throat ailment on 23 December. He died later that day after what was thought to be minor surgery. In some brief comments for the Daily Mail *(26 December 1935), Shaw said Loraine acted "instinctively and very brilliantly," but declined to express any sympathy for his death, "because I am going to die myself shortly." He lived another 15 productive years.*

NOTES

1. Loraine's war service didn't entirely eliminate his theatrical activities, which he maintained by mounting ad-hoc performances with his squadron, including the world premiere of Shaw's *O'Flaherty V.C.* in 1917. See David Gunby, "The First Night of *O'Flaherty V.C.*," *SHAW* 19 (1999): 85–97.
2. "I swam without the slightest hope of escape, solely to put off the disagreeableness of drowning as long as possible . . . " (*CL* 2:708–12, 14 August 1907).
3. Shaw told Loraine that Charlotte's initial reaction to the package was one of shock: "she exclaimed 'He's dead,'" and "was almost turned into a pillar of salt" (Grapes, 21 August 1916). The Grapes Shaw–Loraine Collection contains 20 letters and postcards from Charlotte Shaw to Loraine, mostly of a personal nature (e.g., social engagements and holiday missives).
4. At St George's Church in Hanover Square, London (where Doolittle was married in *Pygmalion*). This was Loraine's second marriage (to Winifred Strangman); his first, to Julia Opp in 1897, ended in divorce in 1902.
5. The auction house is Lawrences Auctioneers (www.lawrences.co.uk) located in Crewkerne, Somerset, about 80 km southeast of Joan Loraine's former home in Porlock, Somerset. The auction was held on 31 January 2014 and in addition to Shaw–Loraine items included Loraine's war archives and memorabilia. A separate auction of Loraine's war archives was held in Oxford in April 2014 (*Daily Telegraph*, 11 April 2014).

6   David Grapes II is Professor Emeritus of Theater at the University of Northern Colorado. (See his brief biography in Acknowledgements, p. x.) His Shaw holdings have led to two previous publications: *"My Dear Watson": Bernard Shaw's Letters to a Critic* (Niagara-on-the-Lake: The Academy of the Shaw Festival, 2017), and *Bernard Shaw's Postmistress: The Memoir of Jisbella Georgina Lyth as Told to Romie Lambkin* (Niagara-on-the-Lake: The Academy of the Shaw Festival, 2019), both edited by L.W. Conolly. (Both books are distributed by Rock's Mills Press, Oakville, Ontario: rocksmillspress.com.)

7   Dan Laurence included five of these in *Collected Letters* (*CL*). Since he did not have access to the originals, he was obliged to rely on the flawed transcriptions in Winifred Loraine's biography. The Shaw–Loraine letters in *CL* are #s 2, 7, 8, 11, and 14 in this edition (in full and accurate transcriptions).

8   While several of the Shaw–Loraine letters, postcards, and cables from the Grapes Collection that are not included in this edition relate to theatrical matters, they do so for the most part only briefly and casually. Others relate to social occasions, meetings, holidays, and travel arrangements. They are selectively quoted from in the headnotes and endnotes to the letters where appropriate. Only one letter from Loraine to Shaw is in the collection. It is a carbon copy of a typed letter dated 24 April 1928 concerning Loraine's proposed tour of Australia (see Letter #22). There is also one letter from Winifred Loraine to Shaw in the collection, and seven letters from Shaw to her. On 8 July 1938 she sent Shaw page proofs of her biography of Loraine, which included what Shaw called his "elucidations," added at the typescript stage in January 1938 and placed in the published text between dagger symbols so as to be easily identifiable, with an explanatory footnote in each case. In a letter of 21 July 1938 Shaw objected to having his comments identified in that way: "to mark them out would make us both ridiculous and suggest that you declined responsibility for my account of the affair." And on 6 August he repeated that he didn't like

"the footnotes and daggers." Winifred Loraine persisted, however. In her book there are seven daggered elucidations from Shaw. For letters from Charlotte Shaw to Loraine in the Grapes Collection, see above, note 3.

9   In *The Unexpected Shaw: Biographical Approaches to G.B.S. and His Work* (New York: Ungar, 1982), Stanley Weintraub writes that Shaw regarded Loraine "as a surrogate son" (175). Weintraub discusses the similar Shaw–Lawrence relationship in *Private Shaw and Public Shaw* (London: Cape, 1963).

10 The punctuation is Shaw's.

11 The Victoria Cross is Britain's highest military honour, introduced in 1856 and awarded for "conspicuous bravery in the face of the enemy." Shaw's O'Flaherty (see note 1) is an unlikely and diffident recipient of the V.C.

12 The Iron Cross is a German military honour instituted in 1813 and reinstated by Hitler in 1939.

13 The aneroid and barograph are types of barometers.

14 A telecommunications code developed in the 1830s by American inventor Samuel Morse (1791–1872).

15 Shaw told Loraine in a letter of 21 August 1916 (Grapes) that "Barker is in St John's Wood Barracks [London], cadet gunner, Royal Horse Artillery, profanely stage-managed by riding instructors, and studying Morse code, cannon trigonometry, and other repulsive parts with no fat in them in the intervals of valeting horses."

16 The date of this bracketed insertion by Shaw, nearly two months later than the date of the letter, is a conundrum.

17 Unidentified, but possibly the country home of Dr William Thelwall Thomas (1865–1927), a Welsh surgeon who practised in Liverpool.

18 An aircraft diving at a steep angle, usually with the engine switched off.

19 When Shaw was insisting to Mrs Campbell that she must create the role of Eliza in *Pygmalion* ("There is no other Liza and can be no other Liza"),

he also named Loraine as "the best" choice for Higgins (*CL* 3:97, 5 July 1912). See Dent 20–26 for Shaw's arguments with Mrs Campbell about Loraine as Higgins, which include references to Higgins doing the role in New York opposite Cissy Loftus as Eliza—which never happened.

20 Loraine had been thinking of the play for some years. On 18 January 1910 Shaw wrote to Loraine to decline his invitation to translate it: it "would take me longer than to write an original play, and I should not do it particularly well," Shaw said. "There is, he suggested, "really only one man who could make a first-rate job of it, and that is Gilbert Murray" (BL Add MS 50559 f 374). The translation used by Loraine for his 1919 production was by Gladys Thomas and Mary F. Gullemard (published by Heinemann in 1898). Shaw gave more advice to Loraine on translation and staging matters for *Cyrano* in a letter of 22 April 1919 (Grapes, and extracts in Loraine 261–62).

21 Shaw was unfailingly ready to forgive Loraine's debts. In a 23 April 1919 letter (Grapes) to Loraine, Shaw told him that there is "no hurry" in repaying debts, and he also reassured him that "in case I die suddenly I hereby declare that your debts to me (if any) are among those which I have by my will instructed my executors not to enforce."

22 In a letter to Loraine approving the production (Grapes, 19 November 1919), Shaw describes the Duke of York's Theatre as "horrid . . . all pillars and bad for sound." He also describes Mrs Campbell's "self complacency" as "very Rainesque."

23 In his *Bernard Shaw's Arms and the Man: A Composite Production Book* (Southern Illinois University Press, 1982) Bernard Dukore drew on this letter (as published by Winifred Loraine), but was unaware of the then-unpublished following letter (#12).

24 Shaw's famous reaction from the stage to the single "boo" amid audience hilarity at the curtain call for *Arms and the Man* at the Avenue Theatre on 21 April 1894 ("My dear fellow, I quite agree with you; but what are we two against so many") is widely recorded (e.g., West 5).

25 A phrase relating to the popular story of grouse causing havoc in a junior officers' mess (gun-room) set for a formal dinner, but also signifying immediate laughter at the very mention of the story without its even being told (as effectively used in Oliver Goldsmith's 1773 comedy *She Stoops to Conquer*).

26 At this point in her transcription of the letter Winifred Loraine inserts lines from a different letter, thus: "There were no laughs in *Cyrano*; and what people miss in Bluntschli is Cyrano's nose. They want the pathos, the defeat that underlay Cyrano from beginning to end. Now, Bluntschli is not a tragic figure and is not defeated; but it does not follow that Loraine as Bluntschli cannot make the same appeal as Loraine as Cyrano. The laughs are not drawing money; they are keeping it out of the house." The lines are actually in the letter of 20 December 1919, though not in the same order (#12 in this edition).

27 One of Winifred Loraine's more arresting emendations to Shaw's letters to Loraine is here: "birds" is changed to "canaries," which Loraine did keep as pets (Loraine 272).

28 Shaw wrote to Loraine the night before *The Happy Ending* opened: "As a matter of business I wish the play a sordid success. As a personal matter I resent your succeeding in any plays but mine" (Grapes, 29 November 1922).

29 On 3 February 1938 Shaw wrote to Winifred Loraine about his meeting with her husband: "My last meeting with Robert was in New York, where he breakfasted with me on the ship (my visit lasted only 24 hours). He had slimmed miraculously and could have played Tanner again quite presentably. I made it a condition of the production of my play *On the Rocks* that he should be engaged for the principal part; but it was too long a one to learn except for a guaranteed Broadway production; and as the play frightened everybody in New York it never came off" (Grapes). A few months later, however, under the auspices of the Federal Theatre Project, *On the Rocks* was produced at Daly's Theatre in New York (15 June 1938).

SOURCES

Conolly, L.W., ed. *Bernard Shaw and Barry Jackson.* Toronto: University of Toronto Press, 2002.

Dent, Alan, ed. *Bernard Shaw and Mrs Patrick Campbell: Their Correspondence.* New York: Knopf, 1952.

Dukore, Bernard F., ed. *Bernard Shaw, The Drama Observed.* 4 vols. University Park, PA: Pennsylvania State University Press, 1993.

Gibbs, A.M. *A Bernard Shaw Chronology.* Basingstoke: Palgrave, 2001.

Langner, Lawrence. *G.B.S. and the Lunatic. Reminiscences of the Long, Lively and Affectionate Friendship between George Bernard Shaw and the Author.* London: Hutchinson, 1964.

Liggera, Lanayre D. *The Life of Robert Loraine. The Stage, the Sky, and George Bernard Shaw.* Newark: University of Delaware Press, 2013.

Loraine, Winifred. *Head Wind: The Story of Robert Loraine.* New York: William Morrow, 1939. [First published as *Robert Loraine, Soldier, Actor, Airman.* London: Collins, 1938.]

Wearing, J.P. *American and British Theatrical Biography: A Directory.* Metuchen, N.J. and London: Scarecrow Press, 1979.

———. *The London Stage 1910–1919: A Calendar of Plays and Players.* 2 vols. Metuchen, N.J. and London: Scarecrow Press, 1982.

———. *The London Stage 1920–1929: A Calendar of Plays and Players.* 3 vols. Metuchen, N.J. and London: Scarecrow Press, 1984.

West, E.J., ed. *Advice to a Young Critic and Other Letters by Bernard Shaw.* New York: Crown Publishers, 1955.

INDEX

Admirable Bashville (Shaw) 11
Afternoon Theatre 11, 13
Ainley, Henry 11, 12, 30, 31
Alcock, John 26
Aldwych Theatre (London) 29, 45, 46
Alhambra, The (London) 47
Ambassadors Theatre (London) 50, 56
Androcles and the Lion (Shaw) 14
Anglo-Swedish Literary Foundation 64, 65
Apollo Theatre (London) 5, 63, 64, 67
Apple Cart, The (Shaw) 66
Arms and the Man (Shaw) 1, 4, 11, 32, 33, 36, 39, 42, 45, 49, 59, 62, 64, 66, 67, 76
Asche, Oscar 66
Avenue Theatre (London) 11, 62

Back to Methuselah (Shaw) 23, 50, 52, 53, 62
Barker, Harley Granville 1, 22, 49, 75
Barrie, J.M. 49
Barrymore, John 52, 53
Bax, Shirley 60
Beith, John Hay 57
Bells, The (melodrama) 34, 35
Bentley's Conscience (movie) 50, 53
Bernhardt, Sarah 32
Bilton, Margaret 17
Black Eyed Susan (Jerrold) 30, 31
Brown, Arthur 26
Burke, Edwin 66
Butt, Alfred 66, 67

Caesar and Cleopatra (Shaw) 26, 52, 53
Calli, Faith 58, 59
Campbell, Mrs Patrick 29, 31, 36, 42, 45, 46, 60, 75, 76

Captain Brassbound's Conversion (Shaw) 5, 60, 61
Casson, Lewis 56, 57
Cavendish-Bentwick, Ruth 29, 30
Chaliapin, Feodor Ivanovich 34, 36
Cholmondeley, Mary 29
Colthurst, Captain & Mrs 30
Columbus, Christopher 28
Common Sense About the War (Shaw) 14, 17
Congreve, William 59
Cooper, Gladys 52, 54, 62
Coquelin, Benoît-Constant 32, 33
Cornell, Katharine 59
Covent Garden Theatre (London) 32
Criterion Theatre (London) 14
Cyrano de Bergerac (Rostand) 1, 2, 30, 32, 33, 34, 39, 44, 64, 65, 76, 77

Daly's Theatre (New York) 77
Dance of Death, The (Strindberg) 63, 64
Days Without End (O'Neill) 68
de Casalis, Jeanne 62
Deburau (Guitry) 50, 51
Devil's Disciple, The (Shaw) 5, 50, 52, 53, 56
Dickens, Charles 38
Don Juan in Hell (Shaw) 1, 27
Drury Lane Theatre (London) 32
du Maurier, Gerald 62, 63
Duke of York's Theatre (London) 4, 32, 36, 42, 47, 52, 76
Duse, Eleanora 47, 48

East of Suez (Maugham) 54, 55, 56, 57
Elder, Ann 17
Evans, Edith 59

Evelyn, Lucie 62
Everyman Theatre (London) 47, 54, 55, 59, 60, 62, 63

Fabian Society 56
Fabian Summer School (Godalming) 57
Fanny's First Play (Shaw) 14
Father, The (Strindberg) 63
Filippi, Rosina 11, 12
Fontanne, Lynn 68, 69
Fripp, Sir Alfred 29
Frohman, Charles 34, 35
"Future of Political Science in America, The" (Shaw) 70

Garrick Theatre (London) 32, 59
Garrick Theatre (New York) 50
Getting Married (Shaw) 1, 11, 30
Globe Theatre (London) 67
Goldsmith, Oliver 12, 77
Grapes, David II ix, x, 3, 73, 74, 75
Great Catherine (Shaw) 22
Gregory, Lady Augusta 29, 30
Grein, Mrs J.T. 59
Guild Theatre (New York) 52
Guitry, Sacha 50, 51
Gullemard, Mary F. 76

Haig, Sir Douglas 27
Hamlet (Shakespeare) 25, 56, 69
Handley-Page Aircraft Company 25, 26
Happy Ending, The (Hay) 57, 58, 77
Harding, Ann 70, 71
Hay, Ian 57
Haymarket Theatre (London) 11, 12, 13, 29, 30, 49, 66
Hearn, James 11, 12
Hearst, William Randolph 70, 71
Heartbreak House (Shaw) 50, 52, 53
Henry IV, Part I (Shakespeare) 27, 60
Henry V (Shakespeare) 27, 36
Henry VI (Shakespeare) 35, 36
His Majesty's Theatre (London) 11, 14, 31, 45, 54
Hoare, Douglas 58
Hoffe, Monckton 52
Holmes-Gore, Dorothy 37
Hudson Theatre (New York) 1
Huntington, Helen 22

Inca of Perusalem, The (Shaw) 22
International Society of Sculptors, Painters and Gravers 27
Irish National Theatre Society 29
Irving, Henry 34, 35
"It's a Long Way to Tipperary" 15, 17

Jackson, Barry 53, 66, 67
Jerrold, Douglas 30
Jones, Henry Arthur 14

Kennedy, Joyce 62
King, Ada 32, 33
King Lear (Shakespeare) 24, 56
Kingston, Gertrude 22

Langner, Lawrence 50, 52, 53, 70
Laurence, Dan H. 3, 74
Lawrence, Gerald 37
Lawrence, T.E. 4
Lawrences Auctioneers 73
Lewis, Cecil 64
Liggera, Lanayre D. 3, 5
Liliom (Molnár) 52, 53
Liszt, Franz 40
Lohr, Marie 11, 12
Loraine, Joan 3, 73
Loraine, Robert
  Accused by Shaw of acting under the influence of morphine 47, 48
  As Bluntschli (*Arms and the Man*) 1, 5, 11, 37–45, 63, 77
  As Cyrano (*Cyrano de Bergerac*) 1, 32–34, 39, 44, 64, 76, 77
  As Tanner (*Man and Superman*) 1, 11, 35, 38, 55, 58, 77
  Australian tour falls through 63, 64, 65, 68
  Borrows money from Shaw 34–35, 54
  Convalescence 15–17, 18, 30, 25
  Correspondence with Charlotte Shaw 73
  Creates role of St John Hotchkiss (*Getting Married*) 1, 11, 30
  Creates role of General Mitchener (*Press Cuttings*) 1, 14
  Death 71
  Final meeting with Shaw 71, 77
  Ill-health 68
  In America 1, 68, 71
  In film 50, 51, 53, 63, 71
  In First World War 1–2

In Strindberg's plays (*The Father, The Dance of Death*) 63–65
In West End plays 14, 32, 49–50, 52, 57, 59
Manages the Apollo Theatre (London) 63, 66–67
Marriages 2, 49
Names Shaw as next-of-kin 2
Nearly drowns while swimming with Shaw 2
Plans to write book about flying 18–21
Returns to acting after war service 32
Rift with Shaw 47
War wounds 1–2, 14, 15–16, 23–24, 25–26, 27–29
Loraine, Winifred 2–5, 47, 52, 57, 59, 64, 65, 74, 75, 76, 77; see also Winifred Strangman
Lorraine-Dietrich (car manufacturer) 50, 52
Lucrece (Wilder) 68
Lunt, Alfred 68, 69
Lyric Theatre (London) 59

McCarthy, Lillah 22, 55, 57
Macdona, Charles 64, 65
Magna (Sudermann) 47
Malvern Festival 53, 66
Man and Superman (Shaw) 1, 14, 34, 35, 38, 52, 54, 55, 57, 59, 64, 68
Man of Destiny (Shaw) 62, 63
Marshall, Armina 70
Mary Rose (Barrie) 49
Massingham, Henry 12, 13
Mathews, Charles 68, 69
Maugham, Somerset 54, 56
Merry Wives of Windsor, The (Shakespeare) 66
Metro-Goldwyn-Mayer 71
Metropolitan Opera House (New York) 70
Misalliance (Shaw) 14
Molnár, Ferenc 52
Morand, M.R. 37, 39
Murray, Alma 62
Murray, Gilbert 76

Nation, The 12, 13
National Theatre (London) 12, 13
Neighbourhood Playhouse (New York) 22
Neilson-Terry, Phyllis 52

O'Flaherty V.C. (Shaw) 73
Old Vic Theatre (London) 56
O'Neill, Eugene 68
On the Rocks (Shaw) 77
Oundle School (Northamptonshire) 32, 33
Overruled (Shaw) 63

Paderewski, Ignacy Jan 11, 12
Palmstierna, Baron Erik Kule 64, 65
Perfect Wagnerite, The (Shaw) 26
Philharmonic Society (London) 12
Pickwick Papers (Dickens) 38
Pinero, Arthur Wing 52; see also *Second Mrs Tanqueray*
Playhouse Theatre (London) 52
Poe, Edgar Allan 11, 13
Political Madhouse in America, The (Shaw) 70
Pomp and Circumstance (Hoffe) 52, 54
Press Cuttings (Shaw) 1, 14
Pygmalion (Shaw) 5, 14, 29, 31, 45, 46, 58, 59, 62, 73, 75

Queen's Theatre (London) 66, 67

Reicher, Frank 50, 52, 53
Reynolds, Paul 21
Ricketts, Charles 27, 28
Richard III (Shakespeare) 27, 31, 36, 38
Richardson, Ralph 62
Rostand, Edmond 32, 35, 67; see also *Cyrano de Bergerac*
Royal Air Force 1
Royal Court Theatre (London) 1, 28
Royal Flying Corps 1, 14
Royal Horse Artillery 75

Saint Joan (Shaw) 50
Sass, Edward 11, 12
Savoy Theatre (London) 32, 63
Schildkraut, Joseph 50, 52, 53
Scott, Lady Kathleen 25
Scott, Robert Falcon 25
Second Mrs Tanqueray, The (Pinero) 52, 53, 55, 58
Shakespeare, William 35, 63; see also *Hamlet, Henry IV, Henry V, Henry VI, King Lear, Richard III*

Shaw, Bernard
   Accuses Loraine of acting under the influence of morphine 47–48
   Advises Loraine on career options 28, 30–31
   Advises Loraine on medical treatment 26
   Advises Loraine on writing a book on flying 18–21
   And Mrs Patrick Campbell 29, 31, 35, 39, 41, 42, 45, 46, 60, 61, 75, 76
   And the Theatre Guild 50, 51, 52, 53, 59, 68, 70
   Attends concert for wounded Belgian soldiers 17
   Declines delayed royalty payment from Loraine 34–35
   Encourages Loraine to play Shakespeare 35–36
   Final meeting with Loraine 71, 77
   Financial acuity 12–13
   On translating Strindberg 65
   Sees Loraine in *Arms and the Man* 37–42, 43–45
   Sees Loraine in *Cyrano de Bergerac* 32–34
   See also titles of individual plays and other works
Shaw, Charlotte 2, 11, 14, 15, 21, 23, 24, 27, 29, 30, 32, 36, 47, 52, 57, 64, 67, 70, 71, 73
She Stoops to Conquer (Goldsmith) 12, 77
Shubert Organization (New York) 68, 69
Silver King, The (Jones) 14
Simonson, Lee 50
Sitgreaves, Beverly 37
Smith, C. Aubrey 29, 45
Stage Society, The (London) 11
Strangman, Winifred (Mrs Loraine) 49, 73
Strindberg, August 1, 63, 65, 67
Sudermann, Hermann 47

Tarzan of the Apes (movie) 47
Terry, Ellen 52
Theatre Guild (New York) 50, 51, 52, 53, 59, 68, 69, 70
This Thing Called Love (Burke) 66
Thomas, Gladys 76
Thomas, Vaughan 50, 51
Thomas, William Thelwall 75
Thorndike, Russell 56, 57
Thorndike, Sybil 56
Tiger Cats ("Michael Orme") 59
Tombeau sous L'Arc de Triomphe, Le (Raynal) 64
Tree, Herbert Beerbohm 11, 45
Tree, Viola 45, 46, 48

Unknown Warrior, The (Lewis) 64, 65

Vassar College (New York) 57, 58
von Richthofen, Manfred 26, 28
War of the Worlds, The (Wells) 26
Way of the World, The (Congreve) 59
Webster, Ben 11, 12, 13
Wells, H.G. 2, 26, 28, 32
Weintraub, Stanley 3, 75
Whistler, James McNeill 27
Whitby, Arthur 37, 38
Wilder, Thornton 68

Yeats, W.B. 29
You Never Can Tell (Shaw) 47, 49

www.ingramcontent.com/pod-product-compliance
Lightning Source LLC
Chambersburg PA
CBHW030913080526
44589CB00010B/285